THE TRAVELLER'S GUIDE TO THE
BEST CAT HOUSES
I N   N E V A D A

Everything You Want to Know About Legal Prostitution in Nevada

by J.R. Schwartz

Box 1810, Boise, ID 83701

ISBN 0-9613653-0-7

J.R. SCHWARTZ
Box 1810, Boise, Idaho 83701

ISBN 0-9613653-0-7

"The gratification of the sexual instinct seems to be the primary motive in man as well as beast."

Dr. Richard von Krafft-Ebing

"Every woman is at heart a rake."

Shakespeare

"A prostitute is a lady in public, cook in the kitchen, and a whore in bed."

Angel, working girl at the
New Sagebrush guest ranch

"Whores give it away, businesswomen sell it."

Gina Wilson,
Madame at Salt Wells Villa

"To be able to fulfill a need of a fellow human being and profit by it, is good business, besides being an act of faith and sometimes charity."

Margo St. James, COYOTE

"O che sciagura d'essere senza coglioni." (Oh what a misfortune to be without testicles).

Voltaire

Acknowledgements:

To the people that helped me put this book together, through encouragement, consideration, time, and more time, without whose support this effort could not have been sustained. Jeff Huber in particular, for his early morning and late night editorializations on the unfinished manuscript, as well as for his humor, absurdity, food and roof. To several other researchers and critics in Salmon, Idaho go my thanks, especially to Ramona at the public library, and to Judy Rife at the Salmon Post Register.

For cover art work, and understanding, Michelle Bottaro, who I feel captured the spirit of the cathouses in her cover illustration.

For maps and additional art work brought in under deadline goes a debt of gratitude to Evelyn Backman Phillips.

To Howard Cain for time and space . . . thanks. To Melissa Hall for help with prepositional phrases. And to Tari Rice, for help with grammatical aberrations, imperfect structuring and wordiness.

Finally, to Mel Del Gallo goes a very special thanks, for without his help this project would not have been completed.

Table of Contents

This book is dedicated to J.C.W., unwavering friend and wine drinking compatriot.

Introduction

Although prostitution has been accepted in Nevada since the days of the Comstock Lode, the legalization of it has been of comparitively recent time. In 1967 the Storey County Commissioners legalized and licensed the first cathouse in Nevada, at which point the Mustang Ranch, and Joe Conforte made history.

Today, prostitution is a thriving, spirited, legal business in Nevada, with 36 *licensed* cathouses operating throughout the state. They stretch from the outskirts of Reno and Carson City, east to Fallon on Highway 50, to Wells on Interstate 80, south to the outskirts of Las Vegas (through Ely and Tonepah), and north on Highway 95, through the deserts and into the mountains.

The cathouses have such exotic names as The Chicken Ranch, the Cottontail, The Cherry Patch, Kitty's Guest Ranch, Mustang, and the New Sagebrush Guest Ranch. Some houses are as small as two room shacks, others as big as hotels.

The women that work in them run the spectrum of age, race, color, and religious preference. Many are extremely religious; others denounced the Bible a long time ago. The names of the working ladies might be Jan, Coco, Keisha, Kim, Cissy, Angel, Kathy, Ashley, or Jennifer. You don't really know, because cathouses are theaters, and the women that work in them actresses. Many girls have stage names, and that's all you will ever know about them. When not performing they have other lives to lead and appreciate their anonymity.

The acts they perform? Anything you want. As Cissy at the New Sagebrush Ranch told me, "I enjoy sex. It's fun. I don't have an orgasm every time, but I do sometimes, and if that's what you want to hear, let me know. If you want me to act like your wife in bed, make a lot of noise, and say that 'You're the best ever,' I'll be happy to do it. Just tell me what you want. I enjoy having a nice time and making the guy feel good."

There are no state laws prohibiting prostitution in Nevada today. Each county has the right to decide whether it wants to have or have not. The only restriction made is that if they do have cathouses, they must be at least 400 yards away from any school or church. In Elko, several years ago, a school was moved when discovered to be located too close to a cathouse.

Currently there are four counties (out of seventeen in Nevada) that have made prostitution a crime: Washoe, Douglas, Carson, and Clark. These are the home counties for Reno, Lake Tahoe and Las Vegas respectively. Their choice was made in deference to gambling interests that were concerned about image, stigmatization, and the time utilization factor. The *beast with two backs* does not gamble, only gambol. So, in Las Vegas and Reno, concerned citizens attempt to keep the sex profile low, and the streets safe for gambling. Accordingly, the experiment has not worked, and the statistics for rape and violent crime in those two cities are staggering.

And what about the cathouses? There the sexual needs of mankind are satisfied without emotional attachment or social embarrassment. It is a business of pleasure, but it is a business, and for many of the working girls there is no room for emotional attachment. Indeed, it may be their downfall.

Prostitution is an occupation for many women, a profession for few. At the cathouse where the girl works it takes precedence over everything. It's what butters her bread, pays for her clothes, and allows her to take vacations on her time off. It takes precedence over sleeping, eating, religious holidays, and having normal relationships.

The shift that the working girl has is usually three weeks on duty, working twelve to sixteen hours non-stop, *partying* anywhere from zero to twelve times a night, or more. There is no real average, no way to compute a real sexual average. There is no norm, no mean, no median in which to compute the average, although anywhere between two and five parties a night might seem standard. Some party more; some party less.

Partying, the euphemism for sex, is a seasonal and biological experience. Obviously the busiest times are when the most men are physically aroused. This could occur during the Reno air races, when the Marines are on leave, during the fishing season, or anytime during ski season. Erections follow no particular time schedule. Holidays encourage arousal. New Year's Eve is usually a big night for most cathouses, and so is the Fourth of July. That means good money for most of the women in those houses, but not necessarily for all of them.

Because sex is not a lottery at these houses, the man can pick and choose his partner as easily as he can order a drink at a bar. He can choose the party and the time. For many girls business is fantastic; for others, some days are not as good as the rest. Some nights are better than others, and many are a complete bust. When a woman is shut out from

3

business she may begin to doubt herself, even feel envy and resentment towards the other girls working in the house. Occasionally there are sales and pep talks to bring the girls out of their sales slumps and doldrums. But ultimately, if that doesn't work, the girl will probably move on to another house, citing slow traffic, or problems with management as the reason for leaving.

Many of the girls have worked in several of the houses over short periods of time, and although they won't go into details of why they have moved on, the answers are pretty basic: Not getting laid enough to support their positive cash flow program, and cynicism.

Or, maybe they weren't logging-in properly, not accounting for all the cash that was coming in, and got caught. It's almost an all cash business. Perhaps they stole from each other. Resentment, envy, and cynicism. Working and living in confining situations can take its toll on the girl, and when she's had enough of it, or is burned out, before she moves on she might be ready to reek vengeance on a system and society she sees as unjust.

Drugs and alcohol? These ladies are no more immune to the temptations than any of us. In fact, their every working hour is involved in dealing with someone who is usually so high or drunk that all he wants to do is perform the most unnatural and bestial of acts upon her, use her like he would Kleenex, then discard her. Sensitivity? This program does not allow for much of it. If anything, the girls need to be as insensitive as possible. It's man's nature to take and discard at will, these ladies are just a part of the theater of it. Drugs and alcohol problems? These women just have to be more careful than most about getting caught. Accordingly, they are regulated and watched much more closely that those who are only there to party.

Licenses are involved: Brothel, liquor, and business. Work

permits are also issued. To the community that means taxes and revenue. The girls must be checked for prior histories and for disease, and be approved before permits are issued to them. And every week thereafter they must submit to gynocological ordeals and then medical examinations. The county sheriff is involved, as well as the county medical examiner, and various other Nevada state health officials. One little slip or mistake can cost the girl her permit, and possibly the cathouse its license. No drugs, no disease, no problems.

Because of their occupation, these women are highly discriminated against. They are at times virtual prisoners of the houses where they have contracted to work, not being allowed out except on their vacations. They're not allowed into the bars or casinos in the county where they are registered; they're not even allowed to mix you a drink at the cathouse where they work. Who knows where their hands and fingers have been? At least they're not going to be on any ice cubes that go into your drink.

The brothel license is too valuable to allow some diseased, drug addicted robbing wench to lose for them! To the owner of the cathouse, it's the only game in town. Thousands of paying patrons visit them annually. The license alone is probably worth more than a million dollars. Add into that the cost of the land, buildings, furnishings, and various inventory, and you are looking at a multi-million dollar business that caters *legally* to the needs, desires, fantasies, wishes, absurdities, and frustrations of more than two million paying partygoers a year. There can be very few mistakes.

When the Marines hit Reno it's full tilt party boogie at Mustang Ranch. And when the "CAGs" arrive in Fallon the same is true at Salt Wells Villa and the Lazy B Guest Ranch. It's true everywhere. Whenever *the urge* arises, whenever it's "Company ladies," it's time to go to work. Time for business, and that may be at 11 a.m. on Tuesday, Saturday at 6:15 p.m., or Wednesday at noon. A nooner, or four in the morning. Whenever *the urge* arises it's time for business. And, the business is pleasure.

The ladies that work in the various cathouses are "independent contractors," which means they set their own price schedules. What you paid for in one house may cost you more, or less, in another house—or they might not even perform the act or service at all. For the most part it depends on them first, and then you. The cost benefit analysis is up to her. Will it be worth the price? It's all negotiable. Is it a service you cannot obtain elsewhere? Is she the most beautiful woman you've seen lately? Is it the first time for you? There's got to be a first time sometime. Are you a salesman just passing though the area, wanting to try something different?

Perhaps you're there for *humanitarian* purposes? Concern for your fellow man? Concerned in that you don't like the way he's eye-balling your ten year old daughter. Maybe he's fondling your pet kitty in a manner that can best be described as suspect. Or, perhaps you've noticed that your prized pet rabbits are suffering from torn rectums and your neighbor is walking around with a fatuous grin on his face, and one hand in his pants! Pederasty or zooerastry? God forbid! But what if? What if this person needs some help sexually?

And how about junior? Is he approaching the age where a little first-hand knowledge and experience will go a long way towards helping him have a healthy outlook on the biological urge? If you and your loved one don't wish to perform in person for him there are cathouses that will allow young men in, as young as fourteen years of age, with parental consent.

What a nice birthday present that might make for some young man. Nothing like the pleasures of a sweet little sugar scoop, a treasure chest of joy on his birthday. *Lingam in yoni?* Enjoyable memories that can last a lifetime. First hand experience, instead of having to read about it in the secrecy of the bathroom, with some tawdry magazine in hand.

The women in these cathouses come in all shapes, sizes, hairstyles, and colors. Maybe you'd like to party with more than one girl at a time? That's always been a fantasy of yours, hasn't it?

All shapes, sizes and colors. Some of those women there are absolute knockouts. Beautiful, gorgeous beauty queens. Peaches and cream. Wholesome and attractive. The kind of stuff you'd like to take home to show momma or the guys. So good looking that you ask yourself why are they there?

Others are average and below. Some are overweight, and look like they eat a lot of food. Others are skin and bones, and look like their meals consist primarily of amphetamines. Pale, flaccid, pasty complexions. Brothel pallor; like they had lived in caves all their lives and never seen the sun. Some have tattoos over all parts of their bodies and remind you of something you saw on a Navy ship. Some look old, used, and dried up. A years supply of K-Y Jelly couldn't help. One walked like she had been bored-out by the man that made the pistons for the Queen Mary. Others walked like wishbones. And still others looked like they had just escaped from a Ukrainian refugee camp. Forty miles of bad back road. Ridden hard and put away wet. Yechh!

But don't ever call them whores because they're not. Anything but that. They're working girls and businesswomen. A whore gives it away. These ladies sell it!

Procedures
&
Etiquette

There are two types of cathouses, parlor and bar. In a bar house a man doesn't have to have sex if he doesn't want to. In a parlor house, sex is what the game is all about, although in many parlor houses you can drink too.

Regardless of which type cathouse you visit the procedures are pretty much the same. You will ring the outside buzzer for admittance and a madam, parlor maid, or hostess will greet you, and let you in. The ladies may already be lined up, or will shortly do so. There may be one girl, five, two dozen or more, depending upon the house, and the time you are visiting. It's a seasonal business, and traffic is much slower in the winter and early spring than in summer and fall.

When the girls introduce themselves to you they are hoping that you will choose one of them. If you can make up your mind immediately they will be pleased, because sex then becomes efficient, and the *time utilization factor* comes into play. You must remember that it is a business for them and you are paying for their time.

When you choose a girl that you would like to party with she will take you into her room where the party will be discussed and negotiated. No sex is discussed in the parlor or at the bar, and neither is money. In her room you can talk freely about anything you want. She will tell you if she will do a certain act, how much money it will cost, etc.

If you can't agree on a price, you are more than welcome to leave without any hard feelings. It's a business, and not all deals are closed. The women are independent contractors and decide for themselves what they will do, and with whom they will do it.

Because they are independent contractors, and not sex slaves to the house, you as a customer must negotiate as to party and to how much you are willing to spend. *PRICE WISE:* It can run from a few dollars to as much as you have (and more), depending on what you're going to be doing together.

It is her prerogative. Requirements and standards as to age, race, gender, color, cleanliness, sobriety, health, and ethnic origins are hers, and they are absolute. She makes the final decision as to who will park his unit where. So, being polite and having lots of money will often compensate for being ugly and rude.

Attitude is very important to the girls. When working a shift they are literally confined to the house for weeks on end. When you stop and consider how long they have to sit around, work, and sleep in the same area you can appreciate the tensions that might build up after awhile. Obviously their patience is tried after working three weeks nonstop, 12 to 16 hour shifts.

You might be her first guy, or the one hundred and seventy fifth during her shift. If you want to make a hit with her, offer to buy her a drink, and put some money into the jukebox (because that's usually the only way it gets played).

You should be there to have fun and enjoy yourself. If you are not there to spend money you shouldn't be there. If you are rude, have a bad attitude, and haven't bathed for awhile, chances are good that you won't be received with open arms.

If you don't see any women that you want to be with be polite about it. If you don't want to go to a room right away with one of them that's fine, buy one a drink and sit and talk for awhile. Be nice about not wanting to be with anyone. Don't feel as if you have to put them down, or that you have to be a sexist. If you are insecure or uncomfortable they will understand. You don't have to be rude or cruel to them. The ladies are there to entertain you and how much they enjoy their work depends entirely upon you. You're more than welcome to shop around, but don't waste their time, because they have better things to do than sit around watching some boring cynical jerk ask a bunch of stupid questions.

Now, when you have succeeded in finding the woman of your choice and have successfully negotiated a party with her in her room, you must next pass inspection. The inspection involves you dropping your drawers, at which point she will inspect your instrument and the surrounding area in microscopic detail. She is looking for something she doesn't want to find, and that you don't want to have: A yellowish discharge denoting some form of venereal disease, or herpes, or little creatures infesting the hairy area surrounding your pleasure weapon. If she finds anything of a questionable nature she will be doing you a service by telling you, and sending you down the road. It means that it's time to clean up your act.

If you pass the inspection and have established a contract, sex will be yours—after you pay her the money. She will take the money, and while you are undressing she will go and "log-in" (give the money to the house for safekeeping, explain the contract, and the time that will be involved), return, and prepare to wash you. The older houses just have "peter pans" and sinks, while the newer cathouses have showers, tubs, and generally nicer facilities to bathe in.

One final rule to remember before you get on (not in) her bed to enjoy sex is that you are not allowed to kiss her on the mouth. You may go down on her and taste the sweet pleasures of her nether region, have her perform oral sex on you (the "French"), come in her mouth, even have her ream your buttock and rectum with her tongue ("Around the World"); but *NO KISSING ON THE MOUTH!* That's because there are unhealthy germs hiding in the mouth. But, it stands to reason that after she's through reaming your anal sphincter with her tongue there just might be a few billion E. Coli germs in her mouth, and you probably wouldn't want to kiss her anyway.

After the sex is performed she will wash you, and herself, maybe see if you want to go again, and then usher you out to the parlor. She will be in her bathrobe at that point, and won't be making small talk. The goodbye from her will be short and sweet. The other girls will be sitting around, and perhaps they would like a shot at your business next.

If you want to stick around for a drink feel free to do so, you've earned it. And besides, who knows? Perhaps that well-endowed sparkling eyed beauty with the pearly pink cheeks and radiant hair sitting in the corner will be the next to arouse your desires?

Reno Area

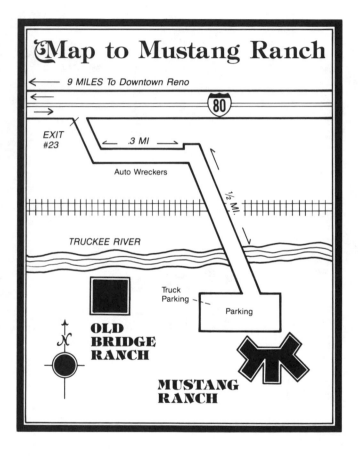

Map to Mustang Ranch

9 MILES To Downtown Reno

80

EXIT #23

.3 MI

Auto Wreckers

½ Mi.

TRUCKEE RIVER

Truck Parking

Parking

OLD BRIDGE RANCH

N

MUSTANG RANCH

Mustang Ranch
Exit 23 (I-80), East of Reno
Storey County
(702) 342-0176 or 342-0531

Mustang Ranch is the most famous cathouse in the United States; maybe the most famous in the world. More than 200,000 men with carnal desires annually trek through her bedroom doors. One hundred and one partying rooms; dozens of captivating girls working twelve hour shifts. Men coming to satisfy every imaginable sexual fantasy in every possible orifice. There is no such thing as an anatomical impossibility; and this is not your ordinary sperm bank. Come by the gallons. Billions of spermatzoa. Deliquescent crystalline aliphatic tetramines $(CH_2CH_2NH)CH_2)_3NH_2)_2$ flagellating up streams of semen actively seeking ovums everywhere. Little do they know they're probably not going to find them.

On September 21, 1990, the IRS tried their best to close the Mustang Ranch down, and succeeded, if but temporarily. But both sides are back open again, still with beautiful women, and good times there for the asking. And Joe Conforte, is still around to help promote the world's oldest sport.

On a busy night 35 to 40 rooms are being worked nonstop by the girls with marines, cowboys, businessmen, sailors, doctors, lawyers and Indian chiefs. Men with pendulous scrotums, turgid penises engorged with blood. As hard as polished steel. Like heat-seeking missiles, cocked and triggered. Immense projectiles, as large as presto logs, smoldering with desire. The women at Mustang have seen every shape and size. You may call it the one-eyed monk, blue throbber, fire poker, majestic spire, magic wand, cyclops, or little chubby. They call it bread and butter.

Security is highly visible at this cathouse, from the guard in the watch tower outside, to the uniformed patrol that makes the rounds of the dormitory wings of this expansive bagnio.

At the Mustang Ranch, volume is so tremendous that a good working girl can gross $100,000 a year for sex. It's known as the "time utilization factor," to her, and depending on what a customer wants it could cost anywhere from two dollars to five dollars per minute, or more. Out calls are especially lucrative for the women.

The turn-over rate for working girls at Mustang, like other houses, varies. Some girls can last ten minutes, others ten years or longer.

Not everyone is cut out to hook. Some girls are better than others. But, there is always a ready supply of girls to step in and fill the void. They call up every day asking for work.

They know that men will always be there, for deer season, the Reno air races, for the camel races in late September, as well as for the snowmobiling races in January.

Three million tourists fly into Reno annually, and Cannon Field is less than ten miles from this cathouse. All cab drivers know where it is, and are more than happy to drive you out, wait while you party, and take you back to town for a fare that's reasonable.

Mustang has orgy rooms, a video room connected to the Jacuzzi, wings of girls' rooms, plus the suites where management stays. The entry is like a grand ballroom, with plush couches and chairs, oil paintings of full breasted women in gilt frames on the walls, and a long clean bar and drinking area.

Drinks were not cheap ($3.00 for a glass of draft beer, and $5.00 for a call drink), but basically the guy isn't there to drink anyway, is he? He could party for the price of a few rounds, and I think that's what they'd rather have him do. But, there is no pressure by the house to go with a girl to her room. If you say that you'd like to have a drink first, that's fine with them.

When you ring the doorbell outside to be admitted, the manager will call out to the girls, "Company ladies," at which point they will line up in a row to be introduced to you when you enter. A dozen or more gorgeous ladies in Danskins, evening gowns, peekaboo lingerie, and spiked heels, all beautifully manicured, and with the finest in hairstyles, just waiting to please you.

When you walk in to that ballroom and see the opulence and lavishness of it, with the young alluring ladies standing there wearing the finest in fashion, the temptations that arise within you can at times become overwhelming. Like a kid in a candy shop, only this one is offering sex candy. And with it no future obligations, no crime ridden connotations, no guilt. Disease-free legal sex, and fun. And you don't have to take her out to dinner first.

When you decide on a girl she will gently take you by the arm and escort you to her room, where all negotiations take place. These rooms are pastel in color, have connecting bathrooms (with bidets), and are decorated in a style of the lady's own choosing. All the rooms are equipped with monitors and panic buttons to make sure no problems arise.

The woman you have chosen to be with is a member of

17

the *piece corps*, and if she is good she should be able to suggest and recommend ideas to the shy, embarassed and naive. You might be into "experimental physics," or nothing more than a 200 calorie exercise in the missionary position. Some women are amenable to almost anything, while others are not.

If you want "Socrates' Pleasures" (anal sex), and the lady of your choice declines, complaining about rectal fissures, lesions, poor sphincter control, foreign bodies in the anus, or perforated anal walls, and you're still determined, ask her to recommend someone else who will oblige you. Many women are not into anal sex in these houses, and believe that the only thing up there should be excreta, but some are, and you just have to inquire.

Love and sex are fantasies to enjoy there. It's like a boarding school for girls, only it's not books that you're going to be studying. These women work. They sell pleasure, and that's all they have to do. They don't have to cook or do the laundry and they don't have to take out the garbage. They only need to satisfy 200,000 men a year sexually. Everything else is done for them. The beautician visits them, as does the designer clothes outfitter. Even the doctor makes house calls. Easy enough, just three straight weeks on duty with twelve hour shifts, working their way through one hundred and fifty guys or so per shift, then taking a well deserved one week vacation before it's time to go back to work again.

Souvenirs from there include t-shirts, decanters, bumper stickers, and even designer sunglasses with the Mustang logo on them.

Storey County was the first to legalize (as opposed to accept) prostitution in America. Joe Conforte was the man who worked the hardest to make it all possible, and Mustang Ranch bears the fruits of his efforts.

Directions: Mustang Ranch is 8.5 miles from the MGM Grand Hotel (located in downtown Reno). Take Interstate 80 east to the Mustang offramp exit #23. Drive straight ahead 3/10 of a mile (past the auto wreckers on your right, and follow the road under the railroad tracks and the Mustang Ranch will be directly in front of you. Enjoy! It's the most famous.

Old Bridge Ranch
Exit 23 - I-80 (east of Reno)
(702)342-0223

The Old Bridge Ranch is another example of what a great cathouse should be: Good management, friendly ladies, comfortable atmosphere and positive attitudes.

David and Ingrid Burgess opened the Old Bridge Ranch in 1984 with 26 party rooms, enough beautiful women to accommodate them all, Jacuzzi, orgy room and a well stocked video library complete with such film classics as "Outrageous Foreplay" and "La Bimbo," starring Alicia Monet a lady who got her professional sex start at the Old Bridge Ranch.

Management is excellent here, from sweet voiced Cathy answering the phones, to Kimers, who makes sure your visit will be a pleasurable one. Kimers was my tour guide when I visited. Super friendly and attractive, she best exemplified what the Old Bridge Ranch was all about—personable ladies who are happy to be there, and even happier to please.

House philosophy and rules are simple here: Make the man feel good, pull your shift, no fighting, no drugs, wear whatever you can make money in (as long as it's not too frontally explicit). Kimers has a term for it, (if you need to know more, inquire within).

The Old Bridge Ranch has a lot to offer. When you first walk into the cozy parlor you're greeted by a friendly hostess who will introduce you to the ladies. Depending on the time of day or night your star search might include Maudy, Jamie, Monica, Leslie, Ricki, or two dozen other ladies.

If you don't wish to immediately trek off to a room, that's fine too. Sit on one of the plush couches and admire the artwork on the walls, watch the two house pets "Spur" and "Doolie" lap around your feet, or head on up to the spacious bar, which proudly pours everything from "Cherry Bombs" (soaked in Everclear) to Jagermeister, with plenty of choices in between.

And if you're into sports, this cathouse offers a double header that can't be beat. A free pass to party with the girl of your choice every time there's a major sporting event on television. With every half-priced drink you buy you receive a raffle ticket good for the drawing at the end of the game. If you win, the choice is yours.

The Old Bridge Ranch is open 24 hours, with girls working different shifts around the clock. The late shift (11:00 p.m. to 11:00 a.m.) will take you down "Horny Lane," while the early shift takes you on a different avenue. There's always a constant influx of new enticing women. Some are "weekenders," college coeds working Thursday through Sunday. Others work two weeks straight, then take a week's vacation. And, if you can't make it in to visit them, they'll do out call service to you . . . anywhere in the world, as long as you have the money and a picture I.D.

The girls that work at the Old Bridge Ranch must first obtain work permits from the county that states their profession as "entertainer." What they offer is probably the safest, most enjoyable sexual entertainment today.

Directions: Take Mustang Exit, cross the bridge, turn right and drive 150 yards. It's on your left with plenty of signs and parking.

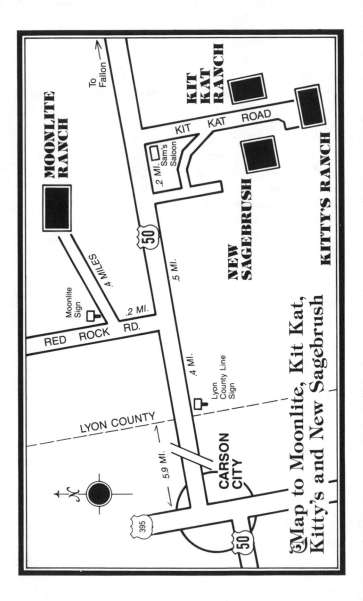

To Fallon →

MOONLITE RANCH

KIT KAT RANCH

KIT KAT ROAD

Sam's Saloon

.2 MI.

NEW SAGEBRUSH

KITTY'S RANCH

4 MILES

Moonlite Sign

.2 MI.

RED ROCK RD.

50

.5 MI.

.4 MI.

Lyon County Sign

LYON COUNTY

5.9 MI.

CARSON CITY

395

50

Map to Moonlite, Kit Kat, Kitty's and New Sagebrush

Lyon County

Lyon County's western boundary line begins about five miles east of Carson City, Nevada. Once you cross that boundary line, antiquated principles, as well as other people's ethics, moral codes, and religious restrictions cease to exist. Instead, Lyon County offers the potential for man to be treated to the finest sexual treasures on the face of the earth. Four legal cathouses exist there, three of which are right next door to each other in an area known as the "Golden Triangle."

The "Golden Triangle" is the home of the New Sagebrush Ranch, Kitty's Guest Ranch, and the Kit Kat Ranch. (The Moonlight Ranch is just down the road). Literally hundreds of thousands of men make the sexual trek to these houses annually, where women are knowledgeable in positions necessary to please. The coital count at these love academies is phenominal, as are the women.

No slouches or hosebags are allowed in here to work. These are not your ordinary trollops, sluts, floozies, harlots, or whores. Here the love business is represented at its finest, with a minimum of sixty beautiful ladies to choose from during sex season, impressive fashion plates, with pleasing skin tones and intriguing looks. And here an attitude exists in the ladies, symbolizing sexuality and free spiritedness. These ladies are confident, radiant, refreshing, defiant. And stylish.

From the "Florentine Olive" silky shadow, to the "Cameo Shrimp" proteined nail glaze they wear, with eye pencil, powder blusher, and lip pencil in between, these ladies radiate beauty.

Eye-filling, well-proportioned bodies wearing the latest in fashion and design, from lingerie with the thinnest of veilings, to hammered silk dresses with rhinestone buttons. Fishnet sheer hose; grafitti stockings; body hugging leathers. Pure silk shirts, and tank tops. The premier lingerie collection in the world is to be found on these ladies, concealing, revealing, and suggesting. No understatement here.

Norma Kamali, Chanel, Armani, and Esprit have all made their fashion statements in the "Golden Triangle." Attractiveness here is an attitude, and these ladies are dressed to kill.

In Lyon County, there can be a certain excitement and exhilaration from having sex with a stranger. Precious lamb-pits, sweet jellyboxes, fun ovens, cock garages, honey pots with submissive limbs . . . whatever phrase you wish to use, sex is meant to be fun there.

New Sagebrush Ranch
Kit Kat Road (east of Carson City)
Lyon County
(702)246-LOVE

Without a doubt Jim and Linda Fondren's New Sage-brush Brothel continues to be one of the finest cathouses in Nevada. Now bigger than ever, with more than 72 party rooms, fantasy suites, a dance floor, two full service bars, Jacuzzis, and more beautiful women than you could possibly imagine to satisfy your every desire, this house has got to be a must stop if you're in the area. And, if you don't want to go visit them, their outcall service to Lake Tahoe, Reno, or Carson City just might be the "E-Ticket" for you.

The owners, management, and working ladies at the New Sagebrush make your visit here a truly memorable one. This modern day multimillion dollar recreational sex spa is clean, spacious, well appointed, and continuously expand-ing. Built from the ground up, it now has two sides to it, with the latest in building codes and comforts. Built without peepholes or panic buttons, your privacy and enjoyment are definitely assured.

And the women working the 72 rooms here are repre-sentative of the most beautiful in the world. Well educated, shapely, sophisticated and friendly. Experienced to say the least.

A few have worked in other houses; many come from

escort services and are tired of being harassed by vice cops. Some are right out of college with degrees; others continue their education *while* working at the New Sagebrush part time. To say that they could teach you a few things would be an understatement.

The ladies that work at the New Sagebrush are some of the most pleasant I've ever interviewed. And the reasons are readily apparent: This brothel has the finest working conditions of any cathouse in Nevada. Each girl has her own room with private shower and bath. In most of the other houses the bathrooms are shared. The girls' rooms at the New Sagebrush are more spacious than any others in the state, each being distinctively decorated by the girl who lives and works in it one week out of the month.

That's another revolutionary thing done here and not elsewhere. The ladies are expected only to work a seven day shift, after which time they can vacation as long as they want before coming back. At many of the other cathouses the girls are expected to work three weeks straight before getting time off.

Job burnout, cynicism and jaded attitudes as evidenced in a few other cathouses is not seen at the New Sagebrush. When you can take a vacation after only one week of work and go spend your money, your attitude is bound to be better than someone who hasn't seen blue sky for three weeks or longer.

Service personnel here also continues to be first rate. This house is under management, not madams (a term Jim and Linda Fondren consider to be archaic). The staff is made up of hostesses and cashiers, not maids. The Fondrens are proud of their first class operation, and can rightfully say that this house probably does more volume than any other brothel in the world. That Jim Fondren was recently chosen as the President of the Nevada Brothel Association is a testament to the dedication and commitment to the positive side of the industry these people work for.

When you ring the bell at the front gate to be admitted several attractive ladies line up, ready to introduce themselves to you. They are exquisitely clothed in a myriad of color extremes. And at the New Sagebrush if you don't wish to go immediately to one of their rooms to party you don't have to. Pressure to party is never applied by the management or the ladies. They don't rush anyone into a party. If you want to just sit and drink that's fine with them because the bar is there to make money too. And it's well stocked and reasonably priced. In fact, they have a "Happy Hour" that goes non-stop from Monday through Tuesday, and well drinks are only one dollar apiece. A person can buy a lot of good will for that kind of money.

On the coffee tables in the parlor are bright yellow pleasure menus, business cards, and matches. The menu can help "break the ice" for first-timers, and is a conversation piece, offering such items as massages, group orgies, water sports, movies, out-dates, fantasy sessions, and much more.

Many first-timers visit here. They also get a lot of guys from Reno and Lake Tahoe as repeat business, as well as high rollers from all over the country. With cab and limousine service available it definitely is first class.

On special occasions the New Sagebrush will have raffles, with the winners receiving free trips to the orgy room with the bright-eyed lady of his choice . . . a woman who is there to make sure you're having a good time.

The New Sagebrush Ranch accepts VISA, MasterCard, and is one of the few cathouses to take American Express. And, the receipt doesn't indicate that you've been to a sporting house.

For souvenirs they have T-shirts, baseball caps, visors, pleasure menus, coffee mugs, matches, and business cards (with a map on the back).

When travelling down the road, and your mind conjures up the possibilities of pleasure, consider this: Two fantasy suites with mirrors almost everywhere, four VIP rooms all styled differently for your myriad theme parties, and three Jacuzzi rooms for wet, warm and wild times. What more could you want . . . only an ATM machine to take care of your financial requirements, and the New Sagebrush has that on site too. Bigger and better. You couldn't ask for more.

Open twenty-four hours a day, with a telephone number that is very easy to remember: Just dial (702)246-LOVE.

Directions: From Carson City drive 6.5 miles east on Highway #50 to Kit Kat Road. You will see Sam's Saloon immediately on your right, as well as a billboard advertising all three cathouses on Kit Kat Road. Turn right and come down 1/8th of a mile, and as Jim Fondren says, they're "the good looking house on the right." That they are!

Kit Kat Ranch
Kit Kat Road (east of Carson City)
Lyon County
(702)246-9975

The Kit Kat Ranch is another one of the fine cathouses in the Golden Triangle offering pleasures and services that are second to none, guaranteed to please the most discriminating of sexual connoisseurs. From the minute you walk into this brothel, take a seat, and wait for the ladies to enter the room for an introduction, you know the time spent here will be worthwhile.

Russ Ernst and Walt Roskaski are the owners of this house, having bought it a few years ago from a nice old lady who finally retired to California after 63 years in the business. They are prominently active in the Nevada Brothel Association (a different kind of N.B.A. ball game), and have spared no expense here, from bringing in exotically beautiful women to satisfy your desires, to hiring some of the finest behind-the-scenes personnel available.

If there were a cathouse Hall of Fame the lady who manages the Kit Kat would definitely be in it: Bridgette. As sharp as they come, with a knowledge and understanding of the business that's almost encyclopedic, Bridgette adds her character, common sense and personality to make a visit here a rewarding experience.

Running the Kit Kat Ranch is like running a small hotel. With 10,000 square feet under the roof, thirty-one working rooms, two kitchens, a beautiful Jacuzzi spa, water bed room with overhead mirrors, two orgy rooms, and twenty-five girls on duty at any one time, logistics are considerable.

Shifts vary for the girls, from whatever is convenient, to whatever is necessary. Some girls like to work noon through midnight, while others like the opposite hours, and variations thereof.

Although the bar is not prominent here, they do have a liquor license and serve only the finest. The reason the bar is not highlighted (as in some other houses) is partially because they don't wish to discourage the 18 to 20 year olds from coming in to enjoy sex (although minors are not allowed to drink in the houses they can experience the other pleasures). Also, Russ and Walt feel that a bar encourages people to hang out—which they wish to discourage.

Asked what problems they have incurred being new proprietors of a cathouse that has three dozen plus female independent contractors working in it, they responded candidly that problems arise from time to time, and occasionally they do have to let some of the girls go.

Sometimes the girls test the management; when they think they can get away with something they'll try it. House rules are pretty basic: Be honest, be good. Try to create a nice atmosphere. They don't condone stealing from clients or from each other, but sometimes it happens. They don't tolerate drugs at all. Their license is worth too much.

Occasionally the girls will "blow out." After having come in together and worked a few months they might grow tired of what they're doing and decide to leave together. Cathouses are no more immune to mistakes and character deficits than any other business that employs so many people. But, because there is too much at stake for management to lose the scrutiny is much more severe, and consequently mistakes are less tolerated. But for every girl that leaves five more apply for the job.

Meeting a girl at the Kit Kat is a little different than at the other two houses on the block. Here you sit down first, and relax for a few moments before the parlor maid says, "Company ladies," at which point they come out and introduce themselves to you—the psychology being that you're more relaxed when you're sitting down. When you do make your selection the girl might follow up by saying, "Would you like to come into my room and play?" (in other houses it oftentimes is more explicit). When an attractive young lady says that to you it's pretty hard to say no.

The Kit Kat Ranch is the oldest cathouse out here. They have been in business since 1968, which was four years before prostitution was legalized in Lyon County. The women in this house are friendly and attractive, and run the spectrum of color and nationality. At the Kit Kat there is no racial discrimination for working girls or for the male customers.

Russ and Walt are proud of their house, from the shocking cupid pink exterior, to the management that runs it. They call it *The Cadillac* of the industry.

The Kit Kat Ranch is open twenty-four hours a day. The girls work fourteen-hour shifts three weeks straight, then take one week off. Between forty and fifty ladies work there through the different shifts.

This house has it all: Jacuzzi, orgy rooms, waterbed rooms, and video rooms. The girls are friendly, and don't put pressure on the guy to party. And the bottled water man says that they use more bottled water than any other house out there. That means lots of visitors. Obviously they're doing something right.

Souvenirs include t-shirts, caps, maps, matches and

business cards. Visa and Mastercharge are accepted here also.

Directions: Drive east on Highway 50 from Carson City about 6.5 miles (which is approximately one mile past the green "Lyon County" sign on the right side of the road). You will see Sam's Saloon on your right, as well as a billboard which announces the presence of the three cathouses on Kit Kat Road. Turn right on Kit Kat Road and drive 1/8 of a mile. The Kit Kat Ranch is the first house on the left. It has a cupid pink exterior that is difficult to miss. Park in the cul-de-sac.

Kitty's Guest Ranch
Kit Kat Road (east of Carson City)
Lyon County
(702)246-9810

Kitty Bono, of Kitty's Guest Ranch, has been on the block the longest. She's been here since 1979, and is now the last madam left in Lyon County. She built her house from the ground up, designed it herself, and has one of the nicest Jacuzzi spas of any of the houses. She has a good perception of what the men want.

Prostitution has been legal in Lyon County since 1972, but like so many other places, it's been around longer than that. Kitty's Guest Ranch has twenty-two rooms, and enough girls working 14-16 hour shifts to accommodate every single one of them. Her girls (she calls them "my children") work three weeks on, then take a week-long vacation (although if they need time off during their shifts they can get 24, 48, or 72 hours, depending upon the urgency.

There are two other cathouses on the block, one on each side of Kitty's and she thinks that's great. "Competition is good for everybody," she told me. "It's good for business because it keeps everyone on their toes."

Kitty's Guest Ranch is easy to spot, especially at night. There's a giant bright red neon arrow in front. She said she got the idea from the Moonlight Ranch, which has a smaller one.

Kitty is a fine lady. She has been in the business a long time—since the early days when Joe Conforte had cathouses on wheels, moving them across county lines to elude police and problems. She used to work for Joe as manager of the old Starlite before opening her own house.

Now she has five or six steady girls working for her year round. She really cares about her "children," and many have been with her a long time. Others come and go, but here too, there never is a shortage of workers.

Kitty's Guest Ranch is a parlor house, and as such there isn't a formal bar. But she has a liquor license and sells moderately priced drinks. She also has outcall dates available with the lady of your choice. And, she never closes, open twenty-four hours a day. Her house is definitely one of the nicer ones to party in.

Souvenirs here include Gift Certificates of $25, $50 and $100 which could make the perfect gift for someone special. Also, t-shirts and baseball hats are on sale.

Directions: The same as for the other two houses out there, just follow Highway 50 (east) 6.5 miles out of Carson City to Kit Kat Road, turn right by Sam's Saloon, and drive down the cul-de-sac 1/8 of a mile. Kitty's Guest Ranch will be directly in front of you.

Moonlight Bunny Ranch
East of Carson City
Lyon County
(702)246-9901

The world famous Moonlight Bunny Ranch is the grand old lady of the cathouses in Lyon County, having been out there since 1956. Twenty working rooms, 12 to 18 girls working 14 hour shifts, 365 days and nights a year. No religious holidays here. And, anything you want you can get, "just like a regular cathouse," the day manager replied.

This was the first house I visited on my journey, and if the manager was protective and guarded in her responses it was because she did not wish to be a part of a new guide book. She had seen one before, and considered it to be "stupid and superficial." Although she felt my presence to be an intrusion into the girls' private lives she was helpful, and suggested to anyone who might be curious to visit and find out for themselves what it's all about. I agree.

My interviews with some of the working girls there went about as well. When I asked one how long she had been there she responded that she "was sprouted there, and was a *brothel sprout*." She may have been a little on the vegitated side at that. Not all of the ladies were as jaded as she was, but a few were there.

Several cars were parked in front of the Moonlight Ranch that afternoon I visited, and obviously this house has an appeal all its own. Business must be good there, and when you realize that this cathouse pays around $25,000 annually for a business license, it better be good.

The girls, incidentally, pay $10.00 to obtain a work permit, and a $5.00 fee annually thereafter. The manager told me that if any girls are interested in applying for work, "Just ring the doorbell."

The Moonlight Bunny Ranch went through a change of ownership in 1991, and now it too is business under management, not madams. New additions to the house include a new bar, hot spa, and a policy that does not include girls doing a "line-up." Here it's more informal; come in, relax, and enjoy yourself. And of course, most credit cards are welcome here.

If there are any restrictions on guys coming into the house to party the day manager told me it's based on the following maxim: "If you're old enough to hold up your peter you're old enough to screw."

Regarding morality, she told me that "prostitution is the greatest thing since T.V." One of the working ladies chimed in that "it's better than T.V.!" Leave It To Beaver???

Directions: 5 miles east of Carson City on Highway 50 you will cross into Lyon County, proclaiming itself with a big green sign on the right side of the road. Within a quarter of a mile on your left is Red Rock Road. (It's the second road on left past Lyon County sign). Turn left on Red Rock and follow 1/2 mile to the end of the cul-de-sac. Park and ring bell!

Fallon
Area

Fallon

Fallon is at the western edge of the "forty mile desert," and for emigrants in the 1850s it meant the hardest part of the trek west was now behind them. The banks of the Carson River (named for John Fremont's scout and Indian fighter Christopher "Kit" Carson) offered the first fresh water the pioneers had seen in some time. Today Fallon is an urban community with a rural atmosphere, the county seat for Churchill County, and home of the Navy's 858th Air Defenses Radar Squadron Group, as well as home for their bombing and target squadrons.

Points of interest for this area include Fort Churchill, built in 1860 to prevent Paiute Indians from interrupting the mail service of the Pony Express; Ichthyosaur Park, where 160 million year old skeletal remains of thirty ancient seagoing reptiles fifty feet long and weighing 10 to 12 tons apiece are found petrified in limestone and volcanic lava; and let's not forget Churchill Counties' two legal cathouses, The Lazy B, and Salt Wells Villa.

SALT WELLS VILLA

"The Best Bordello in the State"

(702)423-5335 Hwy 50 East Fallon, Nevada

Kay

Salt Wells Villa
Highway 50 (Austin Highway)
East of Fallon, Churchill County
(702)423-5335

Prostitution was legalized by the good citizens of Fallon and the Churchill County Commissioners in 1974. Now two legal cathouses flourish just outside the city limits. The largest of the two is owned and operated by Steven Harris, who became the new owner in early 1986.

Salt Wells Villa was a former restaurant, as well as stage coach and pony express stop. (Nearby salt wells used to provide salt for the stamping mills on the Comstock Lode in the 1880s). Although not the most glamorous or romantic cathouse, with its battleship grey exterior and interior, it's still an enjoyable watering hole for cowboys, sailors, and businessmen who want to stop in and have a good time. The ladies that were working when I visited were full of fun and good times. Real characters without any pretensions whatsoever.

Gina Wilson is no longer the opinionated madame in residence there. A possible conflict of interest with the law necessitated her departure from the premises. Gina was best remembered for saying: "Whores give it away, businesswomen sell it." To Gina it was a business complete with pep talks, and the old five point sales plan: Get the customers' attention, then his interest; create desire; get a commitment,

commitment, then close the deal. It worked well for her, and should do nicely for Harris too.

Business there is usually at its best when *the fleet* is in. That's when the Carrier Airwing Groups (known as "CAG's") fly into the Fallon Naval Airstation, just a few miles away. If the fleet is in the girls can see a lot of duty, maybe five to ten customers a night per girl. That means good money for them.

Usually there are four to eight women working at Salt Wells Villa, although in the winter it can slack off a bit. The license fee in Churchill County is $1500 per quarter to run the business, and that allows a house to have a maximum of six girls working. If they want another six girls, they pay $1500 more. The girls themselves pay $7.50 to obtain permits to work.

This cathouse has a Jacuzzi, and "s/m" room complete with riding crops, quirts, and taws, as well as a "stockade" in which the head and hands of the "prisoner" are placed. It's similar to what our forefathers used to imprison their Pilgrim brethren with. A spiked ball and chain, as well as other "toys" were prominently displayed, but all were of a theatrical nature, made in some instances of soft foam rubber. Torture was of the "wet noodle" variety, and if there was any domination it was verbal. The fantasies that take place there are of a humorous nature.

The villa consists of twelve partying rooms, plus a large bar, pool table, video games, and an area for minors (under 21 years) to wait. Guys as young as fourteen years of age are allowed in with their parents' consent (bring a note from home saying it's O.K.!). They also have a waterbed.

I spent more time at this house than in any of the others, and really found the girls to be lots of fun, with wild senses of humor. I think that they could laughingly refer to each other as degenerates without offending anyone. At dinner, two of them were debating the pros and cons of "giving head." Keisha thought it would cause hanging jowls, while Coco was under the impression it would strengthen the neck muscles and give one's face a better tonal quality. All of this took place at the dinner table. Pass the potatoes please!

Once a week the girls go to the clinic for a checkup and medical certification giving them a clean bill of health. Since prostitution has been legalized in Churchill County, venereal disease has been reduced, due in large part to an ordinance that requires the woman to insert (with an eye-dropper-type syringe device) into the customer's unit an antiseptic solution of merthiolate before and after sex. The first time you see the syringe and realize where it's going to go, it might scare the hell out of you! But, it's all quite harmless, and does serve a clinical and psychological purpose, if not romantic one.

Salt Wells Villa has a "Sporting House Menu" with twenty-one items on it, ranging from the "Binaca Blast," to "The Wind, The Rain, and The Lava." They also have a video "training film" showing all of the acts on the menu (except "Alka Seltzer"), if one needs to understand any of it in greater detail!

The women like to experiment there. I was told that they often get tired of the "same old boring positions," and would be happy to suggest a few variations on the theme. Inquire within.

Drinks are moderately priced, and they are open for business twenty-four hours a day. They accept American Express, Visa, and Mastercharge, and have plenty of souvenirs to offer, from shirts and hats to menus.

Very friendly place to visit, from management to the ladies. Even Studley the dog was friendly (he seemed to delight in watching the training film with us, a big fatuous grin on his little doggy face!).

44

Directions: Approximately twelve miles southeast of Fallon on Highway 50 (east) is located the Salt Wells Villa. Seemingly in the middle of nowhere, nothing but desert and snowcapped mountains in the distance; it's on the right side of the road, with a sign in front, (with go-go dancers on it). Have fun.

SPORTING HOUSE MENU

1 BINACA BLAST
2 PEPPERMINT FRENCH
3 EMOTION LOTION
4 WHIPPED CREAM
5 ALKA·SELTZER
6 MOVIE & PARTY
7 DOUBLES
8 TRIP
9 AROUND THE WORLD
10 BUBBLE BATH

11 CHAMPAGNE PARTY
12 SALT & PEPPER
13 HAVING FUN NOW
14 FRENZY EXPLORATIONS
15 SWEET PRESERVES
16 FRENCH SENSATIONS
17 SOCRATES PLEASURES
18 THE APPARATUS DRIVE
19 S&M (B&D)
20 UNINHIBITED FREE FOR ALL

21 THE WIND THE RAIN THE LAVA

SALT WELLS VILLA RANCH

FALLON, NEVADA   ©1983 V.WILLIAMS

46

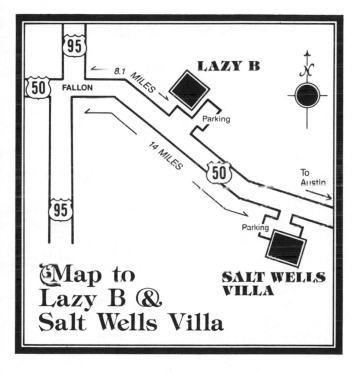

Map to Lazy B & Salt Wells Villa

Lazy B Guest Ranch
8111 Highway 50 (Austin Highway)
Churchill County
(702)423-3221

The Lazy B Guest Ranch is a small cathouse located 8.1 miles southeast of Fallon, on Highway 50 (east). In the summer they have an open house and bar-b-que for the locals to come out and get to know them a little better.

Although it is a small house by comparison, they never close, there are usually two girls always on duty, and the atmosphere is friendly. The bar is comfortable with moderately priced drinks, and there are video machines, pool table and juke box for your entertainment.

The clientele at the Lazy B is mostly Navy personnel. Their bombing run is directly across from here and you often see low flying jets streaking across the desert floor. If any discrimination exists in this house it's what occurs between the officers and enlisted men towards one another, and that's of an elitist nature that can be seen in all branches of the armed services from time to time.

Minors are also welcome there. Guys sixteen years old have a separate waiting room off from the bar where they can meet the lady of their choice (without any stigma or harassment) before partying.

I was told that future plans for development there include a two story Victorian style mansion-recreation spa, with juniper terraces, Jacuzzis, video rooms, and drinking parlors for both men and women. Presently it's "Men Only" at the Lazy B Guest Ranch.

A real character I met there was Angie, an older black maid who had worked at the Moonlight Ranch twenty years ago. She said with conviction that prostitution was a good idea, because "then men don' go roun' rapin' no woman!"

Directions: From Junction 95 and Highway 50 East in Fallon drive east on Highway 50 approximately 8.1 miles. The Lazy B Guest Ranch is the only building out there, on your left, and you'd have to be blind to miss it. There is a big wooden fence to the left of the house, and a cyclone fence in front. A friendly Doberman Pincher by the name of Heidi waits to greet you.

Winnemucca Area

Winnemucca

In 1850, when wagon trains travelling the Emigrant Trail west were crossing the Humboldt River in that area, Winnemucca was then known as French's Ford. The name was changed in 1868 to honor the greatest of Northern Nevada Piaute Indians.

By 1868 the Central Pacific Railroad (controlled by Stanford, Huntington, Hopkins, and Crocker) had reached Winnemucca, and with it came a population of Chinese, miners, Basque sheepherders, ranchers, and railroad men. More than 5,000 Chinese worked as laborers on the railroad, then earning $1.10 a day.

Winnemucca became a terminal and major shipping point for cattle and sheep, as ranchers from northern Nevada, southern Oregon, and northeastern California shipped from this railpoint. The community grew as the needs of ranchers, miners, merchants and gamblers were satisfied.

Houses of prostitution existed, and the spirit of individualism reigned supreme. The people of Winnemucca voted against statehood in the 1864 referendum, serving notice that they didn't need to be incorporated with anyone else. Gold, silver, and cattle had brought prosperity to the cathouses in Winnemucca, all located in a place called "The Line."

Directions: To get to "The Line" drive east on the main street in Winnemucca past the Winner's Inn and Sundance Casino. Two stoplights past the Sundance Casino is Baud Street, where you turn left. There is a Maverick Country Store on that corner. Drive down Baud Street to the stop sign just past Val-U Inn Motel. Now cross Second Street into what looks like an alley, just past Jim's Auto Body Shop. "The Line" starts 200 feet ahead.

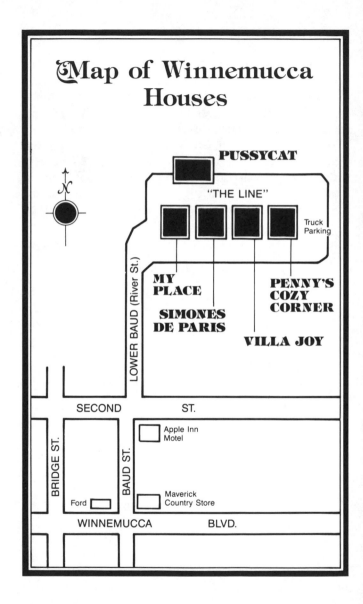

Map of Winnemucca Houses

PUSSYCAT

"THE LINE"

Truck Parking

LOWER BAUD (River St.)

MY PLACE

SIMONES DE PARIS

PENNY'S COZY CORNER

VILLA JOY

SECOND ST.

BRIDGE ST.

BAUD ST.

Apple Inn Motel

Maverick Country Store

Ford

WINNEMUCCA BLVD.

My Place
"The Line," Winnemucca
Humboldt County
(702)623-9919

The first, and friendliest cathouse is called My Place, and is run by Madam Barbara Davis. Eight rooms are working during season, and although they don't accept credit cards, My Place is an enjoyable cathouse in which to spend some cash. It's been there a long time, "As long as cowshit has been on the prarie," I was told.

Known as "Mommy" to her girls, Madam Barbara Davis has a trophy behind the bar which proclaims her to be "The Number One Madam in Nevada," and well she may be. Outspoken, "I provide the happy hunting grounds, the girls are the hunters, and men are fair game" she said, pointing to another trophy given to the house for "Outstanding Entertainment!"

My Place is old, but comfortable. I don't believe that there are any sinks in the bedrooms, so water is bucketed in and out. A Jacuzzi will soon be going in to replace the waterbed, and Madame Davis said, "The balloons are ready to fly again," (in reference to the time when, after having partied with the ladies the guys would come out and pop balloons on the wall, revealing prizes to be given them). The prizes ranged from free drinks, to free parties back in a room with the woman of your choice.

My Place offers outcalls (out of the county), and guys may also spend the night with a lady, who in the morning will provide breakfast in bed, a bubble bath, and lots more loving.

There are always interesting girls here to meet. Last time through it was Amber, Sandy, Cat, Lacy and Tonya. These ladies are unique. They're into therapy and stress relief. If you've got something that needs to be relieved, this could be the stop for you.

Business hours are from 12 noon until 4 a.m., or whenever the action stops. For souvenirs she's got ball point pens. My Place is the first house on "The Line" in many ways. The attitudes and imagination of the people in the house suggest a positive philosophy that business is pleasure. Indeed!

Simones de Paris
Baud Street, "The Line," Winnemucca
Humboldt County
(702) 623-9927

Simone's de Paris Club is right next door to My Place, and here too many changes have occured to the premises and personalities to make this cathouse another enjoyable stop on the circuit.

A new Jacuzzi room has added another dimension of entertainment to this pleasure house, and along with the new ladies now in residence the clientele has *finally* been assured a memorable experience.

The feeling of hospitality extends not only from behind the bar, but also into the party rooms where you can enjoy the company of exciting ladies while viewing the latest in adult video films.

Gone are the rude ladies whose ideas of manners did not quite match mine. When it was Simone's cathouse one lovely lady expressed her verbal and physical capabilities as follows: "I fuck, suck, and dummy up." Cute . . . real nice. She didn't exactly write the book for charm school.

Gone is the air of indifference. It has been replaced by experienced women possessed of warmth and personality. No longer does the shallow hustle exist here, and if the men want to sit and drink when they walk in that's fine, because the bar is there to make money too. It can be enjoyable sitting there, having a drink or two with the lady of your choice, listening to some music first, then going back to her room for some fun and games.

New ownership and management have made Simones a refreshing alternative to dreary cathouse drudgery. They have a new attitude, and a new approach to making the customer feel at ease, from the moment the door swings open until you leave.

Shirts, hats, buttons, and matches are among the list of souvenirs at Simones. But perhaps the best souvenir will be the memory of a pleasurable experience with one of the beauties here. Open twenty-four hours a day, with several ladies to choose from, and they accept numerous credit cards. Enjoy.

The Villa Joy
Baud Street, "The Line," Winnemucca
Humboldt County
(702) 623-9903

The Villa Joy was one of three cathouses owned by Sylvia Binder until recently sold to people who are new to the business but knowledgeable in how to treat their customers right.

The Villa Joy, with a touch of the French New Orleans scene, offers the gentlemen who visit unique entertainment, from eight themed partying mini-suites to a major V.I.P suite complete with hot spa, films, and ladies with looks and callipygian charms that are stunning.

What a difference new management can make. When it was the old Villa Joy it housed oblivious, thick-thighed, overweight women who made it real easy to leave without spending too much money. Lack of sales and success was obviously breeding frustration in them. They were barkers with bad manners, many who should have been sent to obedience training school.

One thing they didn't seem to understand was that they weren't the only commodity on the line. Men with money to spend are also a commodity, especially in an area where there are five different cathouses and a few dozen women to choose from. With competition as intense as it is, politeness and personality will help promote sales better than hostility and hustle. The business is *pleasure,* and far too often many of the girls seem to forget that fact.

And that's why the Villa Joy is so much fun. J.R. has brought in new management, new personalities, and attractive young ladies who know how to treat the customers right.

Now you can linger, laugh, and enjoy yourself with several professionally ambitious and competitive women. All who enjoy sex, all who are capable of weaving delicate webs and enticing you into them with sights, sounds, and fragrances of their sexuality. If you are there to explore the dark veil, to taste the pleasures of the dearest bodily flower . . . the jewel in the lotus, you will not be disappointed. The ladies at the Villa Joy possess all the charms necessary to please.

Open twenty-four hours a day, they never close. Credit cards are accepted, and they have plenty of souvenirs available for purchase.

The Pussycat
Baud Street, "The Line," Winnemucca
(702) 623-9939

The Pussycat . . . a cathouse dating back to the 1800s, and said to be the oldest existing establishment in Nevada.

A Western theme now prevails here, and includes the rustic bar, wooden floors, and an overall country saloon atmosphere swinging with inviting sounds of a charm and quality found in days gone by.

The Pussycat now contains all the elements of warmth and welcome . . . from several enticing young ladies to get your party going, to a modern Jacuzzi spa, and films for your viewing pleasure. There are a dozen partying rooms here, and enough girls with myriad personalities and physical attributes to fill them all.

Once again a change in ownership and management has made all the difference in the world. Virginia has cleaned house, swept out the debris, and gotten rid of the women who seemed to be suffering from anaesthesia sexualis. She took a cold, sterile environment devoid of pleasure and turned it into a laboratory of love, a nest of spicery where instruments of pleasure now play to new music.

Credit cards are accepted, souvenirs are plentiful, and the Pussycat bar is open twenty-four hours a day.

Penny's Cozy Corner
"The Line" in Winnemucca
(702)623-9959

Penny's Cozy Corner is the furthest cathouse to be reached on "The Line" in Winnemucca, but first in the minds of many men who come through here. Her house offers many of the same pleasures as the other ones, but her V.I.P. *Recreational Spa* is one of the finest in the state.

It's its own little version of paradise, complete with a Japanese pagoda, in which sits an exotically fixtured jacuzzi, garden wall murals, cherry blossom tree, floor to ceiling mirrors (at least 14′ high), along with overhead mirrors, plush deep green carpeting, and gold velvet spreads on a bed that is more than comfortable.

A silver champagne set, designer fantasy chair, and other enticements further compliment the split-level room. Plus there are the beautiful women that work here. The ladies that work at Penny's Cozy Corner don't just sell time; they sell a good time. As one lovely lady told me, it was "pennies for pleasure."

Although Penny is no longer with us, her house still offers good times, fine women, and a friendliness that isn't matched elsewhere. At Penny's Cozy Corner, the serious is still laced with the delirious. Penny was a treat, and her house exemplified that. Hopefully, her good will and spirit will live on.

In the bar downstairs the center of attention, and conversation piece is a 4½ foot long walrus penis. That stiff piece of gristle looked like it could be used as a walking cane, or club, and probably gave the pinneped a lot of enjoyment before his demise.

The bar is long and spacious, opposite which are a few tables and chairs. The ladies were plentiful and attractive, and as one said to me, "Without choice there is no freedom." Philosopher queens indeed.

Penny's is a bar house, and comfortable to sit and drink in. The jukeboxes offer the latest in sound, and by offering a couple of dollars for music, and buying a drink or two for one of the ladies you can begin to feel pretty comfortable.

Penny's Cozy Corner is open 24 hours a day, accepts credit cards, and has souvenirs, including matches that say, "Glad you could come."

Directions: In Winnemucca, it's on "The Line," off Baud Street. See map.

Battle Mountain Area

Battle Mountain

Where the hell is Battle Mountain anyway? Battle Mountain has had a history as colorful as any town in Nevada. Indians lived in the territory for at least four thousand years before Peter Skene Ogden, trapper and explorer, representing the British Hudson's Bay Company, became in all probability the first white man to set foot in the area, in 1829. Ogden was twenty-eight years old at the time.

The British policy of the day was simple: "Trap the country dry of beaver," a policy which was intended to discourage American trappers from settling the area. British trappers began exploiting the beaver at a rate of forty to sixty a day, and within four seasons had destroyed most of the beaver population.

In 1845, General John Charles Fremont came through the area, mapping and following the river which he named in honor of the German geographer, Alexander von Humboldt.

The river was the route for westward bound travellers in the mid 1800s. As the migration of emigrants, trappers, and miners continued along this route, hostility by Snake and Shoshone Indians increased. Finally in 1857, in the hills southwest of town, stagecoach road builders fought with

Indians, and that's how the town got its name: Battle Mountain.

Today Interstate 80 parallels much of the Humboldt River, which flows some three hundred miles through Nevada, finally disappearing into the ground thirty miles southeast of Lovelock, at a place known as the Humboldt Sink.

Battle Mountain sits at an elevation of 4,528 feet above sea level, and is located 290 miles west of Salt Lake City, and 217 miles east of Reno on Interstate 80. Today it supports a richly endowed mining and ranching community of almost 5,000 people.

And, although Peter Ogden and the trappers who followed pulled most of the beaver out of the streams years ago a new breed of beaver has supplanted it: The two legged kind! They are alive and well in Battle Mountain's two legal cathouses, the Desert Club, and the Calico Club.

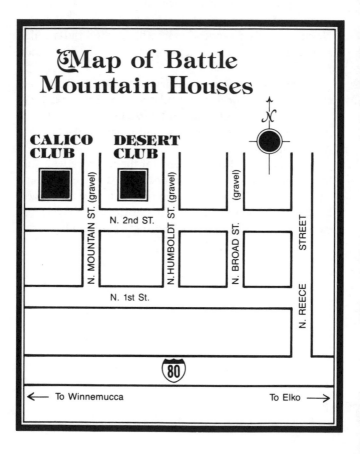

Map of Battle Mountain Houses

CALICO CLUB

DESERT CLUB

N. MOUNTAIN ST. (gravel)

N. HUMBOLDT ST. (gravel)

(gravel)

N. BROAD ST.

N. REECE STREET

N. 2nd ST.

N. 1st St.

80

← To Winnemucca

To Elko →

N

Calico Club & Desert Club
North Second Street, Battle Mountain
Lander County
(702)635-9948; 635-9952

The Desert Club and Calico Club are owned by the same couple, Ginger and Chuck Barrett, and they have a philosophy that works pretty well in their houses: Let the guy get comfortable first. Both houses, located virtually next door to each other, have nice bars to drink at, moderately priced drinks, and offer cordial atmospheres in which to relax. And, there's no pressure to party with any girl. Ginger said, "We find that a lot of our customers come in two or three times before they ever go back to a room. We like to give them the opportunity to get comfortable with their surroundings first; for many men going into a cat house for the first time can be a pretty scary thing." Because of their remoteness from tourist centers like Reno and Las Vegas, almost all of the business consists of repeat customers who expect to be treated right or they just won't come back.

The Barretts purchased the two clubs in August of 1986, buying them from Julie Hickman who had the houses for five years. Chuck, a native Southern Californian, was a citrus rancher turned lawyer in Ventura County, California, and Ginger, a native of Phoenix, Arizona, was a housewife prior to their venturing into the brothel business.

When asked about their lack of experience, Ginger said, "We feel that we can do a better job not having any prior background in this business—we are not bound by any traditions or history...we just do it the way we think is best." Chuck's comment, while more to the point, was, "As an attorney, you are constantly being accused of screwing everybody—at least in this business that's what they come in for. Everything is up front, which makes it a lot easier!"

So far things have worked out well for the new owners who have gone their own way, experimenting with a phone sex operation and a "Fulfill Your Fantasy" program for women who have sexual fantasies about being prostitutes.

The Calico Club is the newer of the two cat houses, with a Jacuzzi, large bar, and lots of hats on the wall collected from patrons. The rule here is: if you get so sleepy or tipsy that your head hits the bar, they get your hat; however, most of the hats were surrendered willingly to the girls by guys who wanted to leave calling cards.

The Desert Club is the older house, dating back to the turn of the century. Over the years rooms were added resulting in a small intimate house with lots of charm and history; but a word of warning: if you are 6 feet tall or more, watch your head—some of the doorways are barely 6 feet.

Both houses have something extra not found in any other house in Nevada: A large framed portrait over the bar of the Madame (Ginger) reclining in the nude. It's worth the trip just to see the picture.

There are six party rooms at the Calico Club, five at the Desert Club; a hot tub at the Calico club and a sauna at the Desert Club. There's a nice variety of ladies working in both houses, and since they are less than a block apart, if you don't see something that appeals to you, you can walk next door and try your luck at the other house. They accept Visa and MasterCard as well as trucker's com checks or the equivalent. About 75% of the business is from truckers, 20% local, with the remainder coming from tourists and hunters.

Ginny and Chuck have written a new "pleasure menu" that includes exotic appetizers, entrees and desserts ranging from a simple massage or breast massage to a "binaca blast french" with myriad pleasures in between. They have also added an introduction to the menu to help explain the procedures to first timers. To help the timid get started, they included a place where you can write the name of a girl you want to meet; the bartender will then discreetly get the message to the girl.

If you wish to spend the night with the girl of your choice in her room, it's possible, from 2 a.m. till 7 a.m. It's more expensive than a motel room—but a lot more fun!

If you are a collector, or just want something to show your friends, both houses have lots of souvenirs including match books, T-shirts, baseball caps, bumper stickers, procelain coffee cups and calendars with the now famous picture of Ginny.

Directions: Take Interstate 80 to Battle Mountain and exit on either the 229 or the 233 exits and follow the business loop into town. Right down town is the only four way intersection, complete with traffic lights that sometimes work. At that intersection turn north onto Reese Street and cross the railroad tracks. Drive two blocks and turn left. The Desert Club and Calico Club will be on your right, less than two blocks away, with signs in front, along with yellow lights and big red beacons on top. The girls take turns on the C.B. radio and can give you directions on channel 19 if you need help.

CALICO CLUB

NORTH 2ND STREET
BATTLE MOUNTAIN NEVADA

Menu

A wide selection of delectable treats for the descriminating gentleman

Appetizers . . .

1. Massage
2. Breast Massage
3. X Rated Movies
4. Hot Tub Party
5. Champagne Bath
6. Bubble Bath
7. Lingerie Show
8. Body Paint

Entrees . . .

1. Straight Party
2. Half & Half
3. 69 Party
4. 69 Party Lay
5. Double Party Show
6. Double Party French
7. Double Party Lay
8. Salt & Pepper
9. Drag Party
10. Dominating Woman
11. Vibrator Party
12. Friends & Lovers
13. All Night Date
14. Out Date

Desserts . . .

1. Hot & Cold French
2. Creme De Menthe French
3. Binaca Blast French
4. Flavored Pussy Party

If you don't see your personal preference listed, Do not hesitate to ask

Sharon's Place
State Route 278, I-80 Exit
Elko County
(702)754-6427

If you take Highway #278 to Ely or Eureka off I-80, take a look about a half mile down on the left side of the road. There's a double wide trailer with lots of entertainment going on inside. They call it Sharon's Place, Nevada's newest brothel, and they claim to have the hottest coffee and the best free showers in the world as an enticement for truckers to stop on by. But even if you're not driving one of the big rigs you're still more than welcome . . . especially if it's more than hot coffee you're looking for.

Carlin had been without a *"social club"* for several years until Sharon's Place opened in the summer of 1989. The idea for Sharon's Place was conceived by Charlie and Sharon Kendricks, two Carlin locals who knew the history of this town from its early railroad days to its present gold mining boom town status. Charlie had the perfect definition of a "social club," and with a degree in Business Administration, was about to provide one. The house sits on 12 acres of land, allowing plenty of room for parking and truck turnarounds. And once inside you have several good looking ladies to choose from, seven rooms to party in, and a thoroughly enjoyable hot spa to wind down in.

This house is open 24 hours a day, accepts VISA and MasterCard, offers T-shirts and hats among the souvenirs they sell, as well as complimentary pleasure menus and matches.

If you have any questions and just happen to be driving by, they constantly monitor CB Channel 19, so "breaker, breaker 18 wheeler" if you want to give them a call.

Directions: Driving east on I-80 you would take the first Carlin exit. At the stop sign turn right (south onto Highway 278 to Eureka), drive about 3/8ths mile up the grade, and Sharon's Place will be on your left. Flashing red light and a prominent sign over the door make it real easy to find. Sharon's is a friendly place with that ridin cowboy spirit. And, for all you bad boys out there that need a good spanking they have "Large Marge" and "Mattress Mary" in the basement, to complete your pleasure needs.

Elko
Area

Elko

In the late 1800s a madam in Elko wagered a crowd that she could walk around the block three times stark naked and nobody would stop her. Some soldiers from the nearby fort helped guarantee her an audience by preceding her with a brass band. Such was the spirit of the times. Today the western tradition is still alive and well in what Lowell Thomas referred to as the "only real cow town left in the West."

Towering Ruby Mountains and blue sky make for an expansive picture. Elko County is larger than the states of Connecticut, Delaware, Massachusettes, Rhode Island, and the District of Columbia combined. It sits at an elevation of 5,060 in the northeasterly portion of the state, and has a population of several thousand people.

Fun and games are unlimited in this year-round playground, from hunting deer to beaver. The Ruby Mountains offer deep virgin powder to skiers and the cathouses on South Third Street offer almost everything but virgins. There are chariot races, hot air balloon races, casinos, rodeos, and sex with five sex farms to choose from, all within walking distance of each other, just off the main street.

Elko was born of the Central Pacific Railroad, and named by Charles Crocker, (who liked to name the way-stations after wild animals), just added an "o" to Elk for this town's name.

Elko is known as the "City of Festivals," and while different events occur throughout the year in Elko, the sex festival is non-stop.

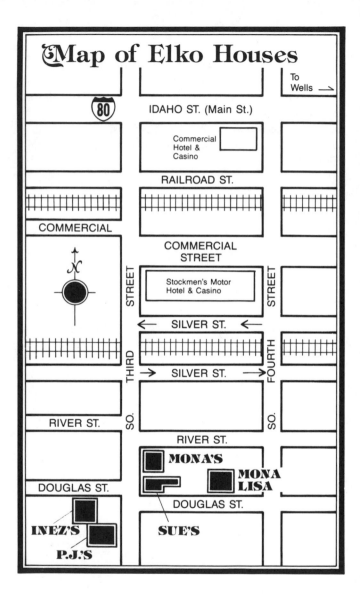

Map of Elko Houses

To Wells →

I-80

IDAHO ST. (Main St.)

Commercial Hotel & Casino

RAILROAD ST.

COMMERCIAL

COMMERCIAL STREET

N

Stockmen's Motor Hotel & Casino

STREET

STREET

← SILVER ST. ←

THIRD

FOURTH

→ SILVER ST. →

RIVER ST.

SO.

SO.

RIVER ST.

MONA'S

MONA LISA

DOUGLAS ST.

DOUGLAS ST.

SUE'S

INEZ'S

P.J.'S

P.J.'s Lucky Strike
246 South Third Street, Elko
Elko County
(702)738-9056

P.J.'s Lucky Strike is still one of the finest houses to visit in Elko, seemingly always changing to stay ahead of the times, but always offering that which time renders eternal, pleasure, companionship, and enjoyment of good times.

P.J.'s is full of entertainment, whether it's visual or visceral, from topless ladies on stage, to full strip tease, and belly dancing. On any given night entertainment can easily be found here.

Once you're inside P.J.'s, friendly lady bartenders are only too happy to pour you reasonably priced drinks, play current and updated Top 20 jukebox music, or offer you the most diversified array of souvenirs for sale in any of the houses in Nevada, from souvenir garters, to hats, liquor decanters, T-shirts, cathouse buttons, coffee cups, note pads, pleasure menus, matches, posters, and books.

But don't forget the ladies: Exotic and erotic, generously catering to most of your fantasies and desires. The possibilities for a good time are innumerable, with foxy ladies like Gina, Hillary, Tara Lee and Anancia virtually guaranteeing you an unforgettable experience. Whether it's sitting at the cozy bar, in the Jacuzzi spa drinking champagne and partying, or sharing bedtime with your favorite lady . . . like Nicole, Chanel, Mai Lee, or Angel, it's all here for the asking.

P.J.'s Lucky Strike is a member of the Elko Chamber of Commerce, and besides being big in community affairs, they're pretty good when it comes to sexual affairs too. Free showers to truckers (along with *almost free* laundry service!). But no matter who you are, businessman, rancher, tourist, miner, or sexually curious man in transit, you'll be treated real well here.

To arouse your curiosity, the "Specialty Menu" includes several nice appetizers, some wonderful entrees, and four enticing desserts. And just like a fine restaurant, P.J.'s accepts major credit cards, including VISA, MasterCard, Diners Club and American Express. However, unlike most fine restaurants I visit, this one never closes. It's nice to know that P.J.'s offers pleasures 24 hours a day.

This cathouse does a good business, for good reasons. They treat the customer right. If you're wondering where to go in Elko this could be the spot for you. It was apparent by watching the influx of traffic through the front door of P.J.'s Lucky Strike that several people were already aware of this fact.

Over the past few years the owners have turned this older looking house into the best on the block. It may be the last house on "the line," but it's first in service, quality and atmosphere. A neon sign in front saying "P.J.'s Lucky Strike" helps you locate it easily.

Directions: The last house on "the line" in Elko, on the right side of the road. See map.

PJ'S

LUCKY STRIKE BAR

"THE BEST LITTLE WHOREHOUSE IN NEVADA"

246 SOUTH THIRD
ELKO, NEVADA

Double Pleasure
VIP Lounge
XXX Movies
Mirror Room
Jacuzzi Party Rooms

Water Sports
Straight Lay
Half and Half
Combo Half and Half
69 Party
Two Girl Show
Two Girl Party
Fantasy Session
Salt & Pepper Party

Desserts
Banaca French
Frappe French
Flavored Pussy Party
Shower Party

Inez's D & D
232 S. Third St. Elko
Elko County
(702)738-9072

New owners from Hawaii have brought a warm and welcome friendliness to a cat house that's been around for a long, long time. Len and Chaly (that's right, Chaly!) became the new owners of Inez's in 1994, and have made it a comfortable pleasure stop worth visiting while traveling through Elko.

It's a cozy place, with a nice Jacuzzi-spa area that has an aquarium and mood lights to set an atmosphere conducive to partying. At the bar it costs $6.00 to buy a lady a drink (of which she gets 50% commission) and at least if you don't plan on partying right away (perhaps you want to shop the four other houses in the neighborhood) you can sit and talk with her for a few minutes, then make up some story as to why you're not ready to party.

Sometimes when you walk into these houses there isn't too much to choose from that you'd really like to spend the time with. A Sierra brown lady named Celeste was working here last time I stopped in. She's got a fantastic figure, with an intellect to match. As Len says, "Stop by, you'll be glad you did." I agree.

Directions: On the South Third Street "Line" in Elko, Inez's D & D is right next door to P.J.'s Lucky Strike.

Sue's
175 South Third Street, Elko
Elko County
(702)738-9962

After a two year hiatus Sue's reopened on December 15, 1990, completely remodeled, with 10 partying rooms including Jacuzzi and V.I.P. room, with plenty of ladies to choose from on most nights.

New owners, new management, and always new ladies make this an experience worth checking out. It's clean, and they offer a variety of souvenirs for sale including hats and shirts, but perhaps the best souvenir might be the memory of a great party here.

Directions: Located across the street from Inez's with a well lit sign on the building. You can't miss it.

175 South 3rd Street • Elko, Nevada • (702) 738-9962

Mona's II
103 South Third St. Elko
Elko County
(702)738-9082

Mona's II is the first cathouse on the left side of South Third Street in Elko. A brown canvas canopy in front protects the patron from inclement weather while he waits to be admitted. An "Open" sign on the corner of the building, as well as Mona's name in front make it easy to find.

Inside this one hundred year old house is a long beautifully restored bar and an inviting array of women. This two story house has twelve partying rooms, and if the walls could talk they'd probably be able to fill volumes of books with anatomical arrangements that Masters and Johnson never dreamed possible.

Down the hall is a Jacuzzi spa that's second to none, and when you party in it a couple of drinks are on the house. With great looking ladies to spend time with, whether it's Mindy, Lyn (one "n" for short n sweet), Shu Shu, Jeanni, Carrie, Bobbie or Angel, pleasure is virtually guaranteed.

If you're a trucker they're on the CB, channel 19 (call for Blue Velvet or Strawberry Rose), and they offer you free coffee, free showers with civilized conversation, and without any pressure or obligation to part with your money. And if money is scarce, they accept Visa and MasterCard too. Parking is no problem either if you're driving an 80 footer . . . there's plenty of it in the back.

A great variety of women work here. As the owner said to me, "If everybody drove Chevrolets it would be one hell of a market." Lyn was a little more poetic when she implied that variety is the spice of life, and they've got plenty of it there. For more than your driving pleasure and poetic curiosity I recommend that you check them out on your next pass through town.

Mona Lisa
357 Douglas Street, Elko
Elko County
(702)738-9923

Around the corner from the rest of the cathouses is the Mona Lisa, located halfway up Douglas Street. A new sign, and new decor help identify this 70 year old cathouse.

And inside, it gets even better. A spacious horseshoe wrap around bar that could easily accommodate you and twenty of your friends. Ceiling fans, designer trak lighting, nice art work on the walls, and fully air conditioned in the heat of the night. Each of the party rooms have TVs and VCRs. Like a fine wine, this house is aging gracefully.

The Mona Lisa offers a Jacuzzi with x-rated films, and no minimum purchase is required on your credit card.

Mona owns this house as well as Mona's II, each with an assortment of attractive women, each open 24 hours night and day. And there are more than souvenirs available here.

Directions: From P.J.'s Lucky Strike you can see the Mona Lisa across on Douglas Street, on the left side. See map.

**Wells
Area**

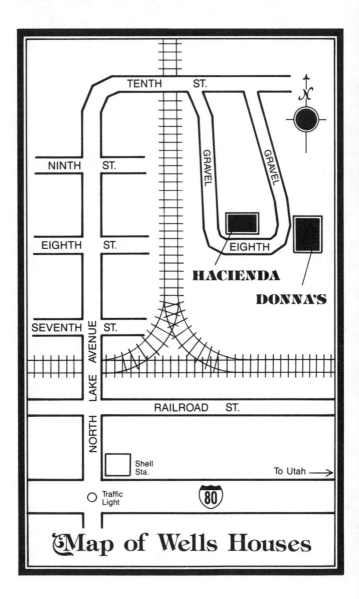

TENTH ST.

NINTH ST.

EIGHTH ST.

GRAVEL GRAVEL

EIGHTH

HACIENDA

DONNA'S

SEVENTH ST.

LAKE AVENUE

RAILROAD ST.

NORTH

Shell
Sta.

To Utah →

Traffic
Light

80

Map of Wells Houses

Hacienda
629 Eighth Street, Wells
Elko County
(702)752-9914

There are two cathouses in Wells. Both have been around many years, and both have seen a lot of action. The Hacienda has been there thirty to fifty years, but inside it's like new.

A bright red sign (50 square feet in size) lets you know that you've arrived. On the sign is the letter "H", engineered to be seen from two miles away, whether you're on the Interstate or U.S. #93.

And if your C.B. is on you might just hear the melodic voices of Spanish Eyes, the Italian Stallion, Silky Susan, or Ramblin Rose beckoning you to come on by the Hacienda Sugar Shack for sweet pleasures most satisfying.

The Hacienda is completely remodeled with new furniture throughout, new beds, new lace curtains with a VIP Room that offers a Jacuzzi, shower and a bedroom area with enough mirrors overhead and on the walls so you can enjoy the visual pleasures that accompany your physical ones, from every possible angle—overhead, diagonally, straight across, above or beneath you. It also has TV and VCR, piped in stereo music, with an ambiance the color of mauve.

Here is the essence of sensuality, removal of the stress

of the road. Eight girl's rooms to party in, with a beautiful lady for every one. Perhaps your desires are for Liza, a blonde international flight attendant with legs that will not quit. Or maybe it's Robin for you, the sensuous one known as Spanish Eyes. Rosa, Vanessa and Dessirré are just as inviting, and your visit here with one or more of these fine ladies will prove that out.

The Hacienda is warm and comfortable no matter what time of year it is outside. From the moment you enter the bar until you leave, pleasure is here for the asking. Great service to truckers, from free showers to free coffee and soft drinks. Full service, including pizza, and sandwiches along with a complete assortment of beverages from "you name it," to Sharp's non-alcoholic beer.

The Hacienda is the finest sexual outpost in this corner of Nevada. Open 24 hours a day, it has a rustic charm combined with contemporary aesthetics and ladies that can't be beat. Music on the jukebox includes country, rock, 50s, soul and Top 40, with plenty to choose from, just like the ladies. And if that's not enough they've got souvenirs, from hats and shirts to dynamic cathouse posters!

The Hacienda is a time out from real life, where pleasure is their total business. Your pleasure is their business. Enjoy.

Directions: In downtown Wells turn at the stoplight where the Shell gas station is located, and head north (towards Idaho). Go across the railroad tracks and follow the road as it loops to the right. Signs are in front.

OPEN 24 HOURS

The
Hacienda
"A Sensuous Delight for any Adventuresome Man"

(702) 752-9914
Wells, Nevada

Donna's
685 Eighth Street, Wells
Elko County
(702) 752-9959

Two hundred feet up the road from the Hacienda is Donna's Ranch, but not for much longer. Soon to be moved and renamed as Apache Wells, this house will boast twenty-six party rooms, VIP suite, hot tub, and piano bar. It will be adjacent to Highway 93 just north of the Interstate 80 intersection, and will offer travellers the convenience of a 200 unit motel, gaming casino, its own radio station, museum, steak house, and limo service to get you around. There will also be a full-service truck stop on site.

But more importantly, there will be lots of girls to play with. The manager of Donna's is a friendly woman named Jeannie (called "Mom" by those who know her). She tries to make sure that your visit is a memorable one, and to that end she makes sure that the ladies that work here are top of the line. Girls like Robin and Jamie and Roxanne. On the CB they're known as "Spanish Eyes," "24 K" and "Luscious Lips." Highly gratifying, with several others to choose from also. So, as Robin says, "If it swells, and you're in Wells, stop on by."

Directions: Turn north at the stoplight by the Shell Station in town and head north across the tracks and follow the road as it veers to the right. It's just past the Hacienda, and has a loop for trucks.

Highway 93 Area

Ely

Ely is the county seat of White Pine County, situated at 6,435 feet above sea level. It was named in honor of John Ely, a miner who in the 1860s bought a mining claim for $3,500 (giving his watch as downpayment), and saw it produce more than $20 million in copper. Nevertheless he died a pauper.

Ely is rich in mining history: At one time it was the most important copper mining area in Nevada; a twenty-five pound gold nugget was found east of town; and garnets can still be collected by rockhounds from nearby Garnet Mountain. Indian petroglyphs, as well as 4,000 year old Bristlecone pines also give this area a sense of history.

And yes, a red light district still flourishes at the west end of town. No longer are there cribs, or four hundred ladies to choose from, but there are three enjoyable cathouses, each occupied by several delightful women to help you pass the time.

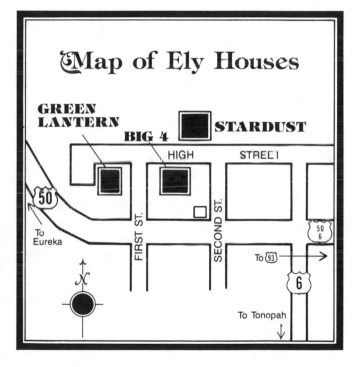

Map of Ely Houses

Stardust Ranch
190 High Street, Ely
White Pine County
(702)289-4569

The Stardust Ranch is a gentleman's social club. The new owners have made significant changes on this house over the past few months to make it inviting, attractive, and well worth a visit if you're in the area.

The Stardust Ranch has been completely remodeled, both inside and out: New exterior, new Jacuzzi, and four bedrooms complete with all the amenities you'll need for a good time, including some of the most attractive ladies this mining town has seen in a long time.

Business hours in Ely are the same for all the cat houses: noon until four in the morning. But, if you'd like to spend a night with the lady of your choice, that can be arranged.

Almost anything can be arranged these days. If you want to put your visit on plastic they take credit cards: Visa and Mastercard. If you want some souvenirs to remember your party by the Stardust has jackets, hats, t-shirts and coffee cups. They also have their own version of Elvis, a four legged character that further enhances any visit to the Stardust Ranch.

Directions: From Aultman Street turn up First Street and drive one block to High. The Stardust is right there, with bright yellow lights flashing a welcome to you.

STARDUST RANCH
(702) 289-4569
190 High St. • Ely, NV
A Gentleman's Social Club

Big 4
High Street, Ely
White Pine County
(702)289-4548

A partially lit sign with an arrow pointing the way announces the presence of this house midway between First and Second Street in Ely. A brick front, and cinder block wall wrap the exterior. This is the Big 4, with new owners Mel and Linda.

Inside is a beautiful bar, behind which is an interesting wall mural entitled *Place Pigalle,* a scene depicting cabaret and brothel life in Paris during the "Roaring Twenties."

The history of this house goes back a long way. Originally the Big 4 used to be a dance hall, and where the cinder block wall wraps around outside there used to be dozens of cribs. In the 1920s when mining was booming in White Pine County there were more than 400 ladies working the cribs. In fact the whole west side of town was cribs.

Directions: From Aultman Street turn onto Second Street and drive up the hill one block to High Street. Turn left and you'll see the Big 4 midway up the block on the left side.

Green Lantern

95 High Street, Ely
White Pine County
(702)289-9958

The Green Lantern is the last cathouse on the hill on High Street in Ely. A once dreary looking front has been replaced by a stone facade. The Green Lantern has a nice bar, moderately priced drinks, a water bed, Jacuzzi, and attractive ladies to choose from.

They also have a pleasure menu that includes such appetizers as Jacuzzi and photo session, Ranch Specialties with outcall dates, water sports and edible undies for Entrees, as well as several desserts that sounded pretty tasty.

The Green Lantern has been "serving mankind since 1948," and obviously they have a lot of experience to fall back on. Fun house. For souvenirs they have t-shirts, baseball caps, and pleasure menus. I think they do a pretty good job promoting.

Open from noon until four a.m.; and they accept Visa and Mastercharge. And at this cathouse exists the possibility of spending the night with a lady of your choice, from 4 a.m. 'til 7 a.m. I doubt that you'd sleep much, but it would probably be an enjoyable sleepless night.

Directions: From Aultman Street turn right at First Street. Come up one block and turn left. The Green Lantern is on the left side of High Street, with a sign in front.

Las Vegas Area

Las Vegas

Las Vegas. Two words conjuring up images of bright lights, instant wealth, immediate gratification, desert landscapes, tourism, and with it temptations, glamour, excitement, and a never ending stream of pilgrims coming to Mecca. The aura of immediate gratification glaring at you, immediate sensual, sexual, physical release.

Neon lights old and new, writing names in the dark dry desert sky, names as colorful as the personalities that stand behind them and who helped write the history of this gambling paradise. From the Flamingo, created by Benjamin "Bugsy" Siegel, to the Thunderbird and thoughts of dread underworld organized crime association. From Moe Dalitz at the Desert Inn, to Del Webb, to Howard Hughes, a man with eccentricities that were more than welcome in Las Vegas, for with them he brought the spectre of legitimacy.

Now corporate faces hold court in the Sands, Dunes, Riviera, Sahara, Flamingo, Stardust, Tropicana, Aladdin, and MGM on *The Strip;* and downtown on Fremont Street, Steve Wynn's Golden Nugget and Barney Binion's Horseshoe cater to the masses, where one more roll of the dice, one more pull of the arm of the bandit, one more spin of the wheel can mean instant gratification for a few lucky souls.

In 1931 the Nevada legislators wrote the "Wide Open Gambling Act," with the hope of bringing investors and big spenders to an area that was considered to be one of the most godforsaken parts of the country. When legislators tacked an amendment onto their bill reducing the residency requirement from three months to six weeks for divorce they perpetuated their notoriety, and *godless* was added to the expletives used to describe them. The *San Francisco Chronicle* wondered in an editorial why they didn't go all out and legalize opium too.

But, their moves paid off and millions of people annually trek to Nevada to spend, and possibly win hundreds of millions of dollars. Today Las Vegas is one of the fastest growing cities in the nation, supplying services and recreation that cannot be as easily obtained elsewhere. Thirteen million tourists flock here yearly to gamble, as well as to watch some of the finest entertainment in the world, from world class entertainers to boxing championships, P.G.A. golf, Grand Prix racing, tennis tournaments, rodeos, hunting, fishing . . . and women, with celebrity status.

You name it, they've got it. Catering to big spenders is what Las Vegas is all about. For those who live to please must please to live. They *rewrote* the book on room service. Las Vegas is tourism, fast living, the night life twenty-four hours a day . . . non-stop excitement, drive, hustle, and release. It's what money was made for: Biological, physical, spiritual release. That means gratification of *the urge,* and don't think the women there aren't aware of it.

Sexuality is an oil they're bathed in, an unctuousness, eliciting responses and creating desires in the men who are there to spend and enjoy. It's a vapor, an unseen presence that permeates all the casinos, from the cocktail waitresses, to keno runners, to the showgirls performing at night. They are the sum total of all their parts, many times dissected:

They are faces, legs, breasts, and hair; a totality of limbs and appendages, the Gestalt of which men would like to devour. They breathe sexuality . . . sensuality. It oozes from them like a spirit, an inner strength, a confidence born of experience and fulfillment. They are beauty, passion, and excitement, catering to your every request . . . almost. In harsher times men would kill for it. Today they will be more than happy to pay for it.

But, inspite of the sexual front constantly bombarding the senses, Las Vegas has cleaned up its act, and promiscuous, available sex for hire is not what it used to be. In Clark County it still is illegal. Streetwalkers are not as visible, parking lot fellatio has decreased in magnitude, fewer call girls are on call, and generally speaking the economy, combined with a new sheriff and law enforcement policy have put a damper on illicit sex in this city. Sexual Reaganomics are in effect, so hookers are not hanging around the street corners anymore, at least not to the extent they used to.

And that's just fine with management. They would rather you leave town bragging about the cards you caught in a Texas Hold-em game, instead of the disease you caught from a lady of the night.

But, if you're in Las Vegas, and determined to enjoy yourself sexually it is available. If *the urge* arises a phone call is all it takes. From that point it's a free limousine ride out there, or a free plane ride if you choose to fly. Three legal cathouses, just minutes over the Clark County line, with dozens of spirited, desirable women willing to satisfy your every desire. North or south of Las Vegas, take your pick. Cherry Patch Ranch, Cherry Patch II or Mabel's Whorehouse. Three of the finest cathouses in Nevada. Take your pick . . . but I suggest you try all three.

110

Cherry Patch Ranch
Near Pahrump
Nye County
(702)372-5251, or 372-5574

Joe Richards says that if you drive north from Las Vegas on U.S. 95 to Highway 160, and turn left you'll soon see a flashing red light, which tells you that you've just arrived at the Cherry Patch Ranch. He ought to know; he owns the place. His license number is #001, and he is pleased to have been the first man in Nye County to have a legal cathouse.

The year was 1976, and since then his little 40 acre community that was once just sand and sagebrush has grown substantially. It's now a town named Crystal, and has about 93 full-time residents, and four full-fledged businesses, including the Cherry Patch Ranch, Mabel's Whorehouse, the Crystal Springs Bar, the Short Branch Saloon, and a gas station and country store just down the road. When asked what inspired him to move away from Las Vegas and the three escort services he operated there, Joe's answer was short and complete: "Money, and not going to jail."

Before Joe Richards moved out there very little existed in the area. The land surrounding his piece of fee simple property is all government owned; he said that his 40 acres is the closest privately held land to Las Vegas, thus giving his cathouse an advertising distinction. Driving north from

Las Vegas it takes about one hour to get to the Cherry Patch Ranch, and you don't have to drive through anyone elses property to get to it—it's all his from the paved road up.

The Cherry Patch has 20 partying rooms, and plenty of enticing young women to occupy them all. The ladies work shifts of three weeks on duty, and one week off. Joe says that they are busy all the time, and there is never a shortage of them. A dozen girls or more call each day asking for employment, knowing full and well that if they are any good at what they do they can make in excess of $75,000 a year (their share)!

The Cherry Patch Ranch offers "damn near anything you want," from simple sex, to the electric chair, with lots of variations in between. They have Japanese baths (hot or cold), *the rack*, and even a dungeon to fulfill your fantasies in. They also cater to, and service women there, as well as have pitbulls, dobies, and German Sheperds on the premises if you're into animal acts (although for the most part they are there for security).

This house is a parlor house, which means that if you want to drink before you party it must be done next door at the Crystal Springs Bar. But once with the captivating lady of your choice in her room you may purchase alcohol to consume with her. They just don't want you hanging out and drinking.

Most of his customers are from Las Vegas, many are Orientals, and most are high rollers. Although many of them take taxis to the Cherry Patch, and pay a nice fare for it, he will limousine or fly you out at no extra charge to the party. The monetary savings alone in cab fares would probably buy you another party or two, so keep that courtesy in mind when visiting this cathouse.

The ladies that work at the Cherry Patch Ranch must possess excellent dispositions, and obviously have to put up with a lot. They have to be able to get along with different people, and they have to be good, in more ways than one. It's estimated that more than 130,000 men visit the Cherry Patch Ranch annually. They probably do more business in a month than most of the other houses do in a year. One working lady had been at the Cherry Patch for six years; another for four years. Like other houses, here too they come and go, some with staying power more enduring than others. The ones I saw had pleasing personalities and they weren't into the hard sell.

The Cherry Patch Ranch has a pleasure menu with about thirteen pages of exotic acts, items, and bonus coupons, along with other souvenirs available for purchase. If you're in the area in search of some fun and entertainment a visit there is definitely a must. Open twenty-four hours a day, year round, they never close.

One thing to remember when you visit Las Vegas looking for a good time is that: ***PROSTITUTION IS ILLEGAL IN CLARK COUNTY!*** If you meet an interesting lady in one of the nightspots you may buy her a drink, you may even offer to take her to dinner or to a show, but the minute you proposition her you have committed a crime. The very thought of it is a crime in Clark County (Las Vegas), and you may be subject to arrest if you have attempted to solicit from the wrong person. It is the thought that is the crime, not the actual deed; You will be in jail long before the act is ever performed if the person you have attempted to solicit is a police officer. Prostitution is seriously frowned upon in Las Vegas, and the statutes are vigorously enforced. So, instead of hassling with unknown factors such as arrest, harassment, entrapment, embarrassment, or even disease, take advantage of the legal, pleasureable possibilities that exist just minutes over the Nye County line.

Now, you can
Experience Your Wildest Fantasies Completely,
Including Costumed Partners And Customed Surroundings. From the Dungeon to the Kings Chambers, Our Fantasy Services have been Created to Totally Fulfill Your Secret Desires.

DOMINANCE, BONDAGE OBEDIENCE TRAINING, SUSPENSION WATER SPORTS, AND MORE

- Enemas
- Spanking Lessons
- Whips
- Paddles
- Belts
- Exotic Bondage
- Dildos
- Devices
- Heavy Leather
- Piercing
- Slave Training
- Rope
- Chains
- Our Famous Rack

Map to Mabel's Whorehouse & Cherry Patch Ranch

To Lathrop Wells
(17 MILES)

95

16

CRYSTAL BOULEVARD

2.4 MI

MABEL'S
CHERRY PATCH

LAS VEGAS

PAHRUMP

HOMESTEAD ROAD

52

8 MILES

178

BLUE DIAMOND

160

Mountain Springs Summit

BLUE DIAMOND EXIT (33)

NEVADA
CALIFORNIA

15

N

STATELINE

NORTH OF LAS VEGAS MABEL'S WHOREHOUSE

A New Standard In Erotic Excellence

People come to our area for one basic reason to have fun. The ways in which people seek their fun are as varied as the human race and, in southern Nevada, we are blessed with being able to fulfill nearly every normal human desire.

In Nye County Nev. north of our own county of Clark with its star performers, glittering casinos and gourmet restaurants that great American institution the brothel is legal and thriving.

Joe Richards' Cherry Patch, located in Crystal, Nev. (about an hour's drive north of Las Vegas), has for years been some mecca for those seeking some adult fun in a controlled, safe and healthy environment.

Last week, in a unanimous vote, the Nye County Licensing Board gave Richards authority to open another brothel in the little community of Crystal, not one inhabitant of which could be found to have anything negative to say about Richards or the Cherry Patch.

The new brothel called Mabel's, is open and ready for business as you read this. For information purposes, we are printing a map of the area, displaying the location of Mabel's and of other significant tourist attractions.

Mabel's is housed in a structure taken from the site of the old El Rancho resort, one of the first hotel casinos built on

for adding a swimming pool and lighted tennis courts.

In addition, the visitor to Mabel's is in for another treat Japanese-style baths with female attendants. The customer is led to a private room, equipped with its own love-tub. Immersed therein, the customer feels tingling fingers over the body, soothing tired muscles with warm scented oils, and is eased into a state of total relaxation. The customer is bathed in Mable's private bubble-bath.

So enjoy the attractions of our area, from shows and casino games on the Strip and downtown, to the love-tub out at Mabel's!

FREE LIMO SERVICE Featuring Japanese Type Baths

PHONE NUMBER
STRAIGHT OUT U.S. 95 North to Highway 160, & turn left. You'll soon see a flashing light
In Nevada Dial (1)
Out of Nevada Dial (702)
(1) 372-5468
(1) 372-5469

MABELS WHOREHOUSE
CHERRY PATCH
RANCH • BROTHEL

LEFT TURN
Only 10 Miles to 160 Turn
Indian Springs
Pahrump
Las Vegas

AH SO SEXY

Mabel's Whorehouse
Crystal
Nye County
(702)372-5468; 372-5469

When asked about sex, W.C. Fields once replied, "I'm not sure whether it's good or bad, but there is nothing else quite like it." If only he had visited Mabel's Whorehouse he would have known that sex is good, very good indeed!

Mabel's Whorehouse is the newest and nicest cat house to be built in the state of Nevada. From the moment you drive (or fly) to this Oriental-themed house located minutes from Las Vegas, you notice the difference immediately. From the Japanese-styled pagoda archway in front welcoming the visitor, to the beautiful women that greet you when you walk inside, you know the experience is going to be memorable.

The artwork on the walls is Japanese, as are many of the exotic ladies that work there. However, fear not if you don't speak Japanese, as there are no language barriers here. *Sex* is spoken universally.

Plush velvet couches to sit on, deep green in color, adding to a warmth and comfort that is heightened by the red brick fireplace containing a warm fire with the light and shadows playing off the open beamed ceiling, further adding a subtle touch to the artworks on the surrounding walls.

From the moment Joe Richards opened Mabel's

Whorehouse in January 1985, he knew he had something special for a clientel that appreciates quality, hospitality, and a touch and taste of the Orient.

The music on the jukebox is predominantly Japanese. All the writing is in Japanese, from the room numbers, to the bar, to the men's room.

There are eight partying rooms now, but plans call for expansion that will include a dozen more play rooms, a salon where men can be attentively taken care of by the woman, or women, of his choice; and where facials, manicures, and pedicures are also available and happily provided by the geishas that reside at Mabel's.

Inside the ladies rooms are home entertainment systems that represent the latest in state-of-the-art technology. Nothing has been left to chance. A stereo system with music piped into each room; televisions in each room that offer you a choice of VCR in-room movies, or 120 ongoing television programs worldwide, courtesy of the satellite dish just outdoors.

And, just down the hallway is a bath and massage salon that you'd expect to find in Japan, not Nevada, with more enchanting ladies of the night there to please you. From Madame Butterfly's "Love Tubs," to showers; what you want is what you get here.

Now here's another nice feature about Mabel's: You don't always have to have sex there. It's not mandatory (like it is in several other cat houses in Nevada). If you want to just sit and drink at the "Far East Bar" that's fine with them. Or, if you want to sit and talk with a lovely geisha in her room, perhaps just have a massage, or a soak in the pool or sauna, perfect.

This house is rated as one of the finest in Nevada, and a quick trip out here will let you know why. First class clientel enjoying exotic, beautiful women. Ladies whose beauty can literally take your breath away.

Want to learn a few Japanese phrases while indulging in some of the finest sexual experiences you'll ever have?

You can bet Berlitz isn't quite the same as this, linguistically speaking! From proper positioning of the tongue, to verbal nuances, you will be working with professionals who know their business. And their business is pleasure, making the guest feel good, turning him on to some of the finest sexual encounters he could possibly hope for.

Fantasy Island? Almost. How many other places do you know of where you can fly your own plane to, park it, walk a few yards, and be inside a sexual paradise that's open twenty-four hours a day, non-stop, year-round? And if you don't fly a plane Joe Richards will be happy to have one sent out to pick you up. And if flying doesn't interest you perhaps free limousine service might. It's all available here, just a telephone call away.

Many people who come to Las Vegas think that prostitution is legal, but it's not. Prostitution is against the law in Clark County (Las Vegas). As such, Mabel's Whorehouse is now the closest legal brothel to Las Vegas. So, if you want to avoid problems think about coming out this direction.

Directions: Mabel's Whorehouse is just a short driving distance from Las Vegas. Take U.S. Highway 95 north towards Reno until you come to Highway 160. Turn left on Highway 160, go five miles, and 6,000 watts of flashing red lights will invite you into *The Valley of the Dolls,* where Mabel's, and the Cherry Patch Ranch are located.

Cherry Patch II

Amargosa Valley
Nye County
(702) 372-5551, or 372-5678

The Cherry Patch II is located 86 miles north of Las Vegas on highway 95, with no dirt roads to drive on. Ultimately it should be the showcase of Joe Richards' sexual empire. It's located in Amargosa Valley (formerly Lathrup Wells) near the Death Valley Highway 373 junction, at elevation 2640 feet.

In the old days people stopped in the area to water their animals. Then came miners, mining, service industries to satisfy needs, ranching and railroads. Borate mining is big business in the area, with Corning Ware owning the American Borate plant outside of town and employing a few hundred people. What started with Charles Lathrup, miner, has grown to an extended community of more than 17,000 people.

The brothel business has been in this town for over thirty-five years. Known a few years ago as the Shamrock, the Cherry Patch II sits on the site of the first railroad station in town. The interior is plush and nicely appointed, with a dozen or so women working in the rooms, ready, willing and able to satisfy most of the requests presented to them by the visiting men. What you have here is an oasis in the middle of a desert.

Joe Richards has gone out of his way to make this more than just an ordinary cathouse since he took over the establishment in 1988. First, it's the closest and easiest to get to from Las Vegas. And it's the only one with its own gas station, full bar and restaurant, and one of the most unique museums of brothel memorabilia around.

On display in open casket is Agnes, a mummified hooker who had stayed too long in the business, I was told . . . a testament to what can happen to "Angels of Mercy" who forget to retire.

But she was definitely the exception. The legal working age in Nevada is 18 years old. Most of the girls working there are young, smooth and sexy, with shapely legs in brightly colored tights, and, to top it off, attractive hairstyles. Find one you like, and take it from there.

The Cherry Patch II is a first rate brothel, and there are plans to add more to it in the future, including a casino and hotel. Getting out there is a breeze, either by limousine, plane, cab, or by your own transportation. The ladies are nice, and the souvenirs are plentiful, everything from T-shirts, caps, sex menus, bumperstickers, and more. Open 24 hours day and night, with credit cards accepted.

Directions: Eighty-six miles north of Las Vegas in Amargosa Valley, near the Highway 373/Death Valley and Highway 95 junction. On the east side of the highway is a huge Union 76 gas station sign, Cowboy Joe's Restaurant and Bar, and the Cherry Patch II. Across the street is the Water 'n Hole. If you're in the area I recommend stopping in.

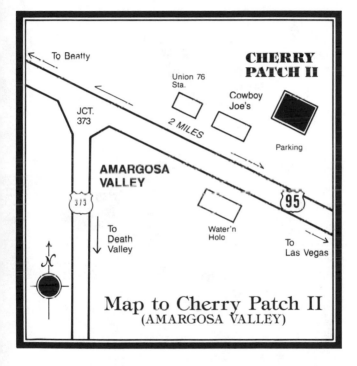

To Beatty

CHERRY PATCH II

Union 76 Sta.

Cowboy Joe's

JCT. 373

2 MILES

Parking

AMARGOSA VALLEY

373

95

To Death Valley

Water'n Holo

To Las Vegas

N

Map to Cherry Patch II
(AMARGOSA VALLEY)

Highway 95 Area

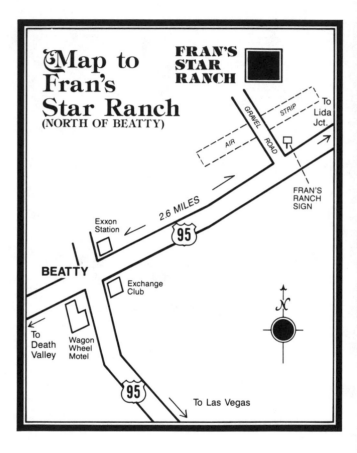

Map to Fran's Star Ranch (NORTH OF BEATTY)

FRAN'S STAR RANCH

To Lida Jct.

GRAVEL ROAD

STRIP

AIR

FRAN'S RANCH SIGN

2.6 MILES

95

Exxon Station

BEATTY

Exchange Club

N

To Death Valley

Wagon Wheel Motel

95

To Las Vegas

Fran's Star Ranch
North of Beatty on Highway 95
Nye County
(702) 553-9986

A plane is "parked" in front by the orange directional wind sock. It's a crashed twin Beechcraft that looks like something Sky King may have flown until he forgot to drop the landing gear while coming in for a visit. Sex can do that to a person. The thought of those beautiful women doing all sorts of nasty things all over your body can oftentimes make a man forget to put down his landing gear. Be careful when flying into Fran's Star Ranch.

Fran's Ranch is located on Highway 95, 2.1 miles north of Beatty, Nevada. A star, formed from white-painted rocks, sits on the hillside and also helps one locate this house from the road.

A few barnwood red outbuildings, a corral, and some horses intermingle along the hillside. Rolling hills and high desert make for a picturesque setting along with sagebrush, cactus and desert, about 90 miles south of Tonopah. In front is a dry river bed, a landing strip for planes, and truck parking with a turnaround.

Inside is a plush parlor with thick lemony cushioned upholstery, and a mountain of coins forming around the coffee table. Fran quoted an old Chinese proverb: "Money on your floor means money at your door." On the walls are a collection of Allan Wood's oil paintings, two of which are entitled "11 p.m." and "5 a.m.," showing various intimate stages of sexual play as the evening wears on in a bar. Another Allan Woods painting hangs from a different wall, showing a Madam and her two girls sitting on a loveseat, a pearl-handled derringer dangling by a golden chain from the Madam's neck as all three ladies smiled. These paintings are classics and worth the visit in their own right.

There has been a cathouse here for forty-five years. Fran has owned it for the past seventeen years. She is a friendly, gentle lady, and obviously has a good sense of humor. The three girls that were working when I visited reflected the good manners and friendly qualities that Fran has.

This is a parlor house and Fran doesn't serve alcohol. She said, "There are seven bars in town, and none sell pussy!" The day they do is the day she sells liquor. She thinks her business should involve other things besides alcohol.

Although there isn't a Jacuzzi here, there are hot springs two miles north, and a dungeon is in the works . . . for theatrical purposes only.

Fran feels that a lot of people are still into romance, and at a cathouse it's an illusion people pay for. But that's not to say people can't fall in love there. If the right guy and girl create the right magic, then who knows? Occasionally Fran will throw a wedding for one of her girls, to show that anything is possible. One of Fran's girls said that she falls in love at least twice a day, and even Fran admitted that she "fell in love once!"

Her card says, "we may doze but never close." Fran's Star Ranch is the social establishment for discriminating gentlemen, located 112 miles north of Las Vegas on Highway 95.

Janie's Ranch

Highway 6, West of Montgomery Pass, Queen Mineral County #702 Montgomery Pass #4 (thru operator) or (619)933-2393

Janie's Ranch west of Montgomery Pass, is located in one of the most beautiful spots in Nevada. Sitting below Boundary Peak (the tallest mountain in the state at 13,140 ft.) and cradled among the trees of the Tolyabe National Forest, visiting Janie's Ranch is like visiting a mountain paradise. The initials "J.R." on the water tank in front let you know that you've arrived.

Madam Janie Curtis is an outspoken woman with much to say. She has seen more in "the business" than many of the other madams, having first "turned out" in Alaska in 1946, being one of the youngest girls on the line. She has had her guest ranch for fifteen years.

This house is the only one where the girls have separate working and sleeping rooms. In every other house the girls must work and live in the same room. Janie feels that that alone would be enough to drive a working girl up a wall! Most people don't like to live, work and sleep in the same room, as it makes life too confining. Also, by separating the living from working quarters she feels that fewer souvenir seekers will walk off with the girl's personal items, such as undergarments, jewelry, pendants, etc.

However, if the guys want souvenirs, she has t-shirts,

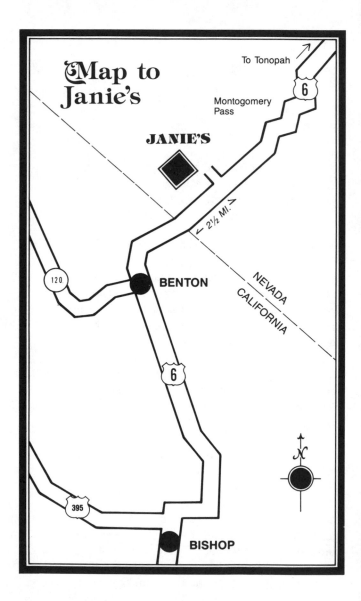

baseball caps, pens, matches, cards, and reminder calendars.

This is a parlor house, so there isn't a bar there. Janie doesn't really think you're there to drink anyway, but if thirst does arise, alcohol is available for the customer, and it's moderately priced.

The working rooms are nicely furnished, all equipped with voice monitors to make sure everything is running smoothly. When I started to ask one of the girls a question (while being given a tour), Janie's melodic voice came back through the monitor from who-knows-where explaining to me that questions of such a nature were not discussed at her house!

The two women that were working when I visited were polite and friendly. There was no pressure to be whisked to one of the rooms in back. They told me that "fishing season" is one of the busiest times for them. (And it seems to last all year round) Also, a lot of men visit during deer season; and they get skiers coming over from Mammoth Mountain, which is about fifty miles away.

Janie's Ranch has a 3,000 foot long runway (about 6,000 ft. elevation), day runway only, so if the urge to fly is there . . . go for it.

There is a beautifully tiled heart-shaped Jacuzzi as well, and although no sex is allowed in the tub, it looked like it would be pretty enjoyable just to sit in.

Also, Janie doesn't accept credit cards at her ranch, but as she explained, she "doesn't sell plastic pussy either!"

Janie said that the majority of the girls today are too wishy-washy; they don't understand where the guy is coming from. A lot of times the guy just wants to talk, and feel as if he is getting to meet the girl. At Janie's Ranch this is recognized, and no pressure is put on the customer to go to the back.

She said that women had more drive five to ten years

ago. Today, a lot of girls come up from California thinking that it's going to be real easy to make lots of money. A lot of them soon find themselves out of the mainstream and drug distribution markets and this can create frustration. Indifference and resentment again. At this point the girls might start stealing from the house, by not logging in properly or reporting all the partying that goes on. Finally the girl goes down the road, either to another house, or to another type of work.

Janie says it's a business, and an honorable one at that. The girls have ethics and morals, and at her house they treat the customer right. The girl's private lives are separate, and when their shifts are done they go off to play, not to hustle some guy for his money in a bar. She believes in a good strong work ethic: Work is pleasure, pleasure then is pleasure.

Open 365 days a year, hours are from 11 a.m. until 4 a.m. To telephone dial the operator and ask for the Nevada Toll Station Operator, and tell them you want: (702) MONTGOMERY PASS #4.

Directions: Janie's Ranch is about two and one half miles east of the California border on Highway 6, coming from Bishop, California. From Tonopah it's a 73.5 mile drive, approximately twenty-six miles west, on Highway 6, from the Highway 95/Highway 6 junction.

Cottontail Ranch
Highway 95 at Lida Junction
Esmeralda County
(702) "Lida Junction #2" (Go through the operator)

At night the shining red light greets you from fifty miles away. A navigational point for pilots, a beacon for wayfaring strangers, reaching out to guide them across the barren land toward their ultimate destination and rendezvous with sexual pleasure. A lighthouse in a sea of sand, lighting the way for seamen to cross this vast ocean of desert, leading them from the *nowhere* to the *now here*, to this sexual epicenter and oasis . . . to Beverly Harrel's world famous Cottontail Ranch.

The humble exterior of this cathouse located 40 miles south of Tonopah may lull you into thinking that not much can exist inside. But don't be mislead, for the Cottontail Ranch contains some of the most experienced and knowledgeable women on the circuit. Wise to the ways of the world. Intriguing, sensuous, ambitious, and gratifying.

The possibilities for having an extraordinary time in this desert sex palace are more than plentiful. Imaginative, professional women with standards of excellence and attractiveness guaranteed to arouse any latent sexual proclivities the customer might have.

There are no moral hangups at the Cottontail, and almost anything goes. Knowledgeable ladies with plenty of ex-

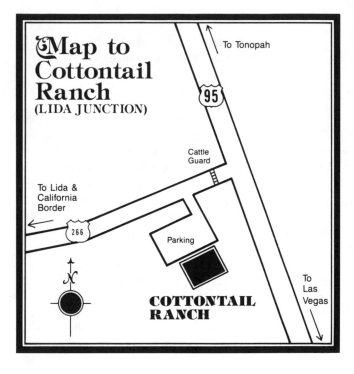

Map to Cottontail Ranch
(LIDA JUNCTION)

To Tonopah

95

Cattle Guard

To Lida & California Border

266

Parking

N

To Las Vegas

COTTONTAIL RANCH

perience and hindsight . . . more than willing to open up to suggestions.

Adventure. The other side of life. Perhaps you'd like a tempting young lovely with spiked heels to tred up and down your back, or to tie you up with yarn and have you beg for mercy. Maybe just the old missionary position with a variation or two on the theme? Whether it's the old *hoo ha*, or a whiff of the Spring Wind, these temptresses can accomplish the task. Sex is the common denominator in this fun cathouse, with ladies that are promiscuous and pleasing.

Every possible theme, from innocence to nastiness. From ladies who look like secretaries (but who won't be taking shorthand), and where "dictation" takes on a new meaning, to girls who can answer the question of "Where's the Beef?" in several different ways. All competitive in bed sports.

The madam of the house is Beverly Harrell, and she sees herself as the #1 Madam in America. Her book, *An Orderly House*, gives lots of insight into the brothel business, and also expounds her cathouse philosophy.

The Cottontail Ranch has been in operation since 1967, a long time, and Beverly probably does more business through mail order than many cathouses do in person. For souvenirs she has medallions, shirts, aprons, baseball caps, honorary certificates of achievement, autographed copies of her book, matches, and much more.

And always an abundance of ladies to choose from, with exotic names like Ashley, Erica, Silver, and Lee; a myriad of colors, physical attributes and personalities. Their desires are yours, from the moment they introduce themselves until it's time for you to leave.

This cathouse has it all, from a well stocked bar in front, to the Jacuzzi spa, to the bedrooms that have soft red lights that turn on when you do (to enhance the mood and also let you know when time is up). The airstrip out back is long enough to accommodate small jets if you wish to fly in, and the partying goes on here non-stop, twenty-four hours a day.

A visit here is a must for a good time with fun ladies who can be more than appreciative of your presence.

Directions: Forty miles south of Tonopah on Highway 95, and at the Highway 3 junction (Lida Junction) is the Cottontail Ranch. Bright red lights at night in the desert help guide you, as well as flashing white lights, and signs all around the cathouse. Enjoy yourself.

Tonopah

Tonopah came into being when miner Jim Butler allegedly picked up a rock to throw at one of his obstinate mules and found the stone to be unusually heavy for its size. Assays confirmed that he had indeed discovered silver ore, and in May of 1900 Nevada's last big silver boom began. The Tonopah boom coincided with the last waning of the Comstock Lode in Virginia City as the center of political and economic influence in Nevada. Ultimately more than $150 million in silver and gold was taken out of the mountains surrounding this community.

Tonopah is a Shoshone Indian word meaning "a small spring." After 1900 the area was anything but that, ultimately boasting a population in excess of 20,000 people, scores of saloons, casinos, hotels, and a red-light district that rivaled any in the West. The largest and most impressive of "houses" was the Big Casino, a dance hall and brothel occupying a square city block in the middle of the sporting district. Although the Big Casino has long since disappeared, there are a few old-timers and sourdoughs that could tell you of an evening or two spent there with "taxidancers" and other ladies of the night.

Silver in the ground finally played out in 1920, and Tonopah quieted down to a present day population of about

4,000 people. The mining that takes place today is for molybdenum in an open pit owned by the Anaconda Company just outside of town. The economy is further sustained by farming and ranching, and by assorted top-secret military projects at the vast Tonopah Test Range Site east of town. The MX missile system is being developed for that region of the state.

Tonopah is the county seat for Nye County, which is the third largest county in the United States. It is located in a hilly terrain, at an elevation of 6,000 feet, 239 miles southeast of Reno on U.S. Highway 95, 207 miles northwest of Las Vegas, and 168 miles southwest of Ely via U.S. Highway 6. Stark landscapes, sage and blackbrush, as well as high mountain desert cradle this town that has seen the likes of Jim Butler, Wyatt Earp and Jack Dempsey calling it home at one time or another.

And yes, prostitution is alive and well in Tonopah. The house is called Bobbie's Buckeye Bar.

Bobbie's Buckeye Bar
7269 Highway 6, Tonopah
Nye County
(702)482-9984

Bobbie's Buckeye Bar, madamed by Bobbie Duncan, has been in business at least thirty years under Bobbie's direction, and who knows prior to that. The building is old, and as if to emphasize that fact, there is an historical landmark sign behind the bar which proclaims that on Feb 4th, 1783, "This was declared the first house condemned in America!"

A friendly atmosphere exists from the moment you walk in through a door that, unlike most other houses, is not locked or controlled electronically. The exterior of the house is cupid pink in color. Inside is a long, *long* bar leading towards the "Caution: Passion Zone" sign, behind which are several working rooms. Behind the bar are various trophies and plaques for outstanding achievement and community service. White paneling wraps the bar area, and gives the impression of a spacious double-wide trailer.

Although Bobbie doesn't promote with t-shirts, baseball caps or business cards she has a constant influx of customers from the MX Test Site project, as well as miners, and guys travelling through town who probably stop in knowing that this is a very low profile house, with no pressure to go to the back and party.

If you just want to sit, drink, talk, and listen you can.

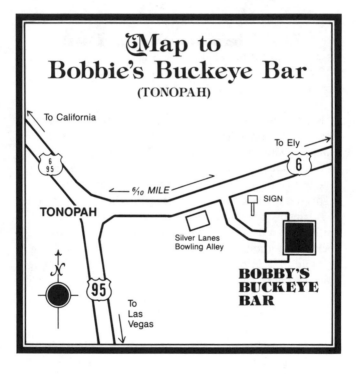

Map to
Bobbie's Buckeye Bar
(TONOPAH)

To California

To Ely

6
95

6

⁶⁄₁₀ MILE

TONOPAH

SIGN

Silver Lanes
Bowling Alley

BOBBY'S
BUCKEYE
BAR

95

To
Las
Vegas

The music on the jukebox is Top Twenty, and Country & Western, (including Hank Williams and Cow Pattie). However, another sign behind the bar stating that "pussy is better than hamburger" can go to work on your subconscious, especially with an attractive lady like Michelle sitting by your side.

If you wanted to pick up a souvenir from Bobbie's there are for sale a limited edition of decanters sculpted by Doug Pickens, an artist who did a collector's edition of decanters for twenty of the houses in Nevada. Bobbie's decanter shows a mini-shorted girl with an inviting look, sitting on a mining car that is ready to head into a mine shaft.

Bobbie is probably one of the last of the old breed of madams, and not much has changed in her house over the years. Still no Jacuzzi, and credit cards are not accepted. Under a sign saying "credit department" there is a statuette of someone giving the finger, so don't even bother to ask! Drinks are relatively cheap, and if you are in the area it's a friendly place to visit. She is open from 12 noon until 1 a.m., or whenever business stops.

Directions: In Tonopah at the junction of Highway 95 and Highway 6 east (which leads to Ely) follow Highway 6 one half mile until you pass on your right the Silver Lanes Bowling Alley. Bobbie's Buckeye Bar is next door, with a sign well-lit on the hillside on your right. Total distance from the junction to her front door is less than 8/10ths of a mile, and the cupid pink exterior, as well as red light, and "open for business" sign all the more reinforce your awareness.

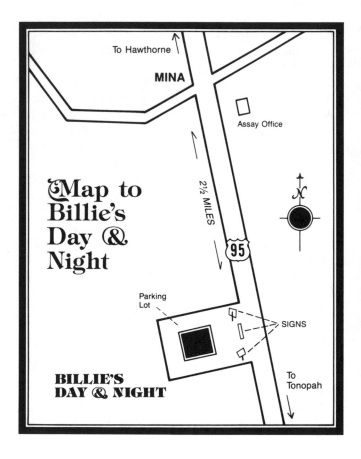

Map to Billie's Day & Night

Billies Day & Night
South of Mina, Mineral County
No Telephone

Billies Day & Night is a small little hole-in-the-wall two and one half miles south of Mina, on a beer-bottle strewn section of Highway 95. In need of much repair (a screw driver through a hasp lock was holding the door shut) it's been in existance since 1975.

Usually there are a couple of girls on duty, but when I arrived they were in Hawthorne at the clinic for their weekly examinations. I sat and talked with Homer the bartender, for awhile, had a beer and waited for the ladies. He's a real character.

This house does not have a telephone, but they are always open for business. No souvenirs or credit cards accepted, and if you're driving too fast you'd probably drive right by because it's small and hardly noticeable.

The bar is small, maybe half a dozen stools, ten or twelve drinking glasses of myriad shapes and sizes (with very few matching), but it still only costs you a dollar for a can of Bud.

A sign behind the bar says: "To all the virgins in the world, thanks for nothing." I felt the same about the place.

History

A Brief History of Prostitution

It's been around as long as the primates have. Female chimps have been observed assuming *the position* in exchange for food from their male counterparts. In humans, bartering sex in exchange for other considerations has been a way of life since Adam shared his apple with Eve. And, the first cathouse was probably built by the first carpenter who saw the benefits of having a women's warm body by his side, to keep him company and give him pleasure at night.

In the early days of civilization the Babylonians required every woman to submit to intercourse with a stranger at the temple of Ishtar. The man would signify his choice by throwing a coin into the lap of the woman he desired. At this point prostitution was a solemn religious duty (in the service of a goddess). In less civilized society prostitution was performed as a sacrifice of virginity, and as a puberty rite to earn a dowry. It was also a fertility rite. Plenty of reference is made in the Old Testament to the proliferation of prostitution in Palestine, describing those women of ill-fame as infesting the wayside in distinctive dress and bearing. Ultimately the economic aspects had come to supplant the spiritual motives, and with that came licensing and control. Rules and regulations were established to preserve order, keep the public safe, and identify the women.

The Egyptians, who invented lipstick, may have been the first to play the game successfully. Egyptian prostitutes who specialized in fellatio wore lipstick. By reddening their lips they made their mouths seem more like the vulva. Any women who painted her lips was thereby advertising the nature of her professional specialty. Cleopatra was said to be one of the best fellatrices in her day, reportedly doing one hundred Roman nobles in one night. How many times she reapplied her lipstick is unknown!

Solon, one of the seven wise men of ancient Greece (c. 550 B.C.) established state controlled houses of prostitution. A cathouse at that time was called, appropriately enough a *Dicteria*. The neighbors to the west did not immediately emulate the Greeks, trying instead to preserve female virtue as long as possible. However, Cato (240 B.C.), in Rome, implied that it was all right for men driven by lust to visit brothels, rather than molest other men's wives.

Ultimately the prostitutes in Italy were also placed under strict government control. They had to register in the city where they worked; they had to wear distinctive clothes; they had to dye their hair, or wear yellow wigs; and, they were taxed, as well as subjected to fines. Whether the regulations were instituted to facilitate the customer's search, or to stigmatize the women remans unclear.

By the 1100s prostitution was pretty well recognized as serving a useful purpose in society: First, it constituted a source of revenue, and secondly, it constituted a source of pleasure. As such it was further protected and licensed. In Europe it thrived: *Bordel, Frauenhauser, Dicteria, Stew, Maison de Tolerance, Bagnio, Wa-Tzu, etc.*

But, with the rise of sexual promiscuity came disease. *Infirmitas nefanda,* the German's Disease, the French

Disease, the pox, syphillis, V.D. Whatever it was, it wasn't enjoyable to have, and something needed to be done.

The 1600s brought the Industrial Revolution, Enlightenment, and Humanist Reform. The Reformation brought radical change to sexual morality. No longer were the clergy to indulge while listening to confessions (solicitato ad turpia). And attempts were made to bring order to the streets. But exploitation and squalor brought on by the industrialization of Europe induced apathy and need to many women. Economic exploitation forced many to the streets to survive. Prostitution was for many women the only occupation open to them. Society had made life cheap and reckless.

America, in the early 1800s was a land of few men, and fewer women. In the West the lack of women was even more noticeably acute. There were explorers, adventurers, trappers, traders, and miners, but no white women. Men out there suffered from severe loneliness. In the West they all knew who the first white woman would be, they just didn't know how much she would cost.

Her name was Jane Barnes, and she was to become the first white woman to set foot in the Northwest. She was a "play for pay" lady from England who agreed to be "le compagnon du voyage" of Donald McTavish (one of the owners of the North West Fur Company). He was a very wealthy man, and had a good eye for pelt. Compensation for Jane amounted to her being outfitted with an unlimited wardrobe, as well as being assigned an annuity for life to make the journey. Marriage was not a part of the plan for McTavish. Together they arrived at Fort George (formerly named Astoria) at the mouth of the Columbia River in the Oregon Territory on April 24, 1814, the first white couple in the Northwest.

Jane Barnes was described as a "vain, dressy, loose-boned

ex vestal of engaging address with an eye to the main chance." She was immediately in demand. The son of the Chinook Indian chief offered her 100 sea otters if she would consent to become his mistress. He tried further to entice her by stipulating that she wouldn't have to carry wood, or dig for roots, and that she could smoke as many pipes of tobacco as she wanted. Nevertheless, she declined his offer, stating that she had no use for a man with a flat head and a body besmeared with whale oil. Thus spoke the first "Independent Contractor." From that point on women of "easier virtue" were in the vanguard of every move westward, and they knew their worth.

By the mid 1800s the West already had its share of legendary madams. In Denver there was Matti Silks (a nineteen year old madam), and Branch Brown. Together they published what may have been the first traveller's guide to cathouses for their customers, and for commercial purposes. It was a pocket-sized guide to the "pleasure resorts," entitled "The Red Book." It advertised parlor houses with "23 rooms, 15 boarders," and the serving of fine cigars, liquors and wines to "gentlemen seeking relaxation." It said strangers were welcome. As the mining boom continued its westward trek so did the women, with California and Nevada becoming the next watering holes.

In the spring of 1849 there were fewer than twenty white women in San Francisco, and the following census year showed that less than eight percent of all inhabitants in California were women. The law of supply and demand was about to be tested. It was a women's world out West. Some were treated like royalty while others were not.

There was "Madame Bulldog." It was said that she weighed 190 pounds naked, usually was, and acted as her own bouncer in her bar. There was "the Waddling Duck," a hideously fat singer who was billed as the only female in the world who could sing in two keys at once! On the Barbary Coast there were the Dancing Heifer, the Galloping Cow, the Little Lost Chicken, Madame Mustache, and many more, too numerous to mention. Yet as comical and absurd as some of these ladies were, for awhile they were the only game in town.

Ah Toy arrived in San Francisco in 1850, and was to become the most famous Chinese courtesan in the city's history. By 1851 there were hundreds of women in California attempting to fulfill the demands for companionship, but it was a task far beyond their numerical ability to provide. Streetwalkers, prostitutes in houses, along with courtesans working exclusive clienteles had soon marked the Barbary Coast (present day North Beach in San Francisco) as the sink of moral pollution. The acute shortage of women had made the West a profitable haven for women of easy virtue, and a jingle was coined to mark the occasion:

> *"The miners came in '49*
> *The whores in '51*
> *And when they got together*
> *They produced the native son"*

Although they were considered *soiled doves* by many, the positive contributions they made were immense to the taming of the West. Prior to their presence normal feminine and domestic associations were dismally lacking. To the miners they were like gold, a combination of beauty and scarcity of commodity. In the predominantly male society of the West they were very much appreciated. For starters men now bathed and combed their hairs before going into a fandango or saloon, in the hopes of better impressing the female. The silken-haired representatives of the fairer sex were a pleasing sight to men who worked sixteen hours a day in mud holes, and whose main fuel and comfort had been ethyl alcohol. The saloons with women in them became their new homes. Women were providing a civilizing influence to an otherwise drab and crude existence.

Nevada was the last Western frontier to be conquered. It had been a land bridge for people going to California. It was thought to be barren, devoid of beauty, and scarce of women. It was a lawless land and Godless. But it was rich in minerals, gold, silver, and copper, and the people that were to conquer it were as rugged and defiant as any that you would find on earth.

Nevada became a land of opportunity for those who gambled and won. It represented freedom and social equality for every nationality, but more importantly for women because they were needed the most. In 1860 there were twenty men for every woman in Nevada. She was companionship, and sexuality, and she was there to tame the beast.

For the price of a few drinks she would dance with a man in a hurdy gurdy dance hall. For a few dollars more she could be hired for a longer time and for a different purpose. The rest of America may have thought the Nevada Territory to be Godless but Nevadans didn't care. What others thought about, Nevadans did. The bestial urge, and economics ruled the territory. Money and sex, pure and simple. Supply and demand. These men wanted to be serviced and entertained. The women were there to do it.

Virginia City. During the last half of the 19th Century the Comstock Lode and Virginia City dominated the Western scene. Eight hundred million dollars in gold and silver was pulled out from beneath her streets. It was the greatest bonanza in precious metals ever. Men worked below the surface in 130 degree temperatures where dynamite caps oftentimes blew too soon, where bodies fell hundreds of feet down mine shafts, and where the daily ordeal offered to crush, smother or roast them alive 1200 feet below the surface of the earth. Perhaps if they were lucky they would only be mangled or maimed. Life was real cheap in the mines, and at the end of the shift the miners just wanted to get drunk and get laid.

In 1859 Julia Bulette was the most famous woman in Virginia City. She was one of the few unattached females in a booming community of hundreds of miners. Her fee was at times reported to be $1,000 per evening. But she too was to die broke, a victim of murder in 1867.

By 1863 Virginia City had a population in excess of thirty thousand people (its present day population is less than eight hundred). It was the second largest city then west of Chicago, with "a red light district superior to any other, from Denver to the Coast, both in size and in variety and amiability of its inmates."

There were many different levels of prostitution by then in Virginia City. The term itself was a euphemism for "fallen ladies," the "fair but frail," and by 1863 there were a few hundred of them in town. The different levels of prostitution went from the lowest slave-trade involving Chinese women–in sweatshops and cribs, being paid one dollar per customer, to street walkers and drug addicts selling their bodies, to the house parlor prostitutes (who were making ten to twenty dollars per customer), and the higher echelon courtesans who usually were with only one man a night. Caroline "Cad the Brick" Thompson was the most famous madam in early Virginia City history.

Besides those types of red light ladies, there were also actresses who would come to town, and under the guise of being theatrical stars, would *perform again* after the curtain had gone down.

If a woman had any ability at all she could make a fortune as an entertainer in Nevada. During her performance appreciative men would shower the stage with gold and silver. She would play to large audiences in public, and to more intimate ones after.

Ida Menken was one such actress who visited Virginia City in the early 1860s. Mark Twain would write that she symbolized infinite desire. Thousands of men wished to violate her body nightly, but only the wealthier ones did. Lotta Crabtree also came to town, baring her legs, singing love ballads, and smoking cigarettes on stage. She was young and attractive, and had the ability to drive men crazy with desire. These women were defiant, free spirited, and sexually liberated.

By the mid 1860s prostitutes were the second largest group of working women, after domestics, in the state. They were an uncommon commodity, non-traditional, and independent. They were there to satisfy a need. The need was companionship, physical and psychological. If they were overpriced nobody was complaining. It was Babylon. Gold bricks would shower the stage. Mining certificates worth fortunes were given them. All for pleasure, gratification, and satisfaction of the biological urge.

By 1875 the mining boom had peaked in Virginia City, and prostitution diminished as an enterprise. A new order of women was beginning to supplant the first. Wealth had brought nicer ladies, who in turn brought manners and a semblence of order. They also brought a sense of home, stability and family, and they didn't want their security threatened by prostitutes. With this new respectability came the demand that less attention be paid to the "soiled doves" out there.

The prostitute was now ridiculed and ostracized from the community. The service she had provided was soon to be forgotten. There were economic retributions against her, and the men who had previously worshipped her as a godsend now rebuked her. The hypocrite had spoken.

Nevada lay economically dormant from about 1900 to

1930, as mining camps came and went. Most of the mines had played out (although there were occasional success stories). The land seemed barren again, and the country was in the throes of depression. Nevadans soon tired of their poverty and alkalai dust and realized they needed something to stimulate their economy. So, in 1931 they legalized gambling, and made divorce easy. And prostitution was acceptable once again. Although they were to incur the wrath of the moral world the Nevada legislators didn't care. They had always believed in individual liberty, the right to do with your body as you pleased. And, they also believed in money.

In Las Vegas it was known as "Block 16," located a few blocks north of Fremont Street. Housed in cribs were women of all varieties and breeds: Japanese, Mexican, Italian, Black, White, etc. In Reno it was in the Riverside District, off North Second Street, and it was known as "the stockade," or "bullpen." It consisted of two low continuous red brick buildings, each housing about forty cribs. The architecture was identical. Door and window exterior with a lane between (a promenade for men), and at the end was a bar blaring honky tonk music.

The girls in the cribs would either sit in their windows or stand by their doors trying to lure men into their rooms. They weren't allowed to leave their crib to greet visitors. Their names were printed on cards above the doorways. Inside were the minimal amounts of furniture necessary to conduct business: Stove, chair, bed, dresser, table, and maybe a radio.

In those days the girls paid a rent of two dollars a day for use of the crib, and kept the rest of the money for themselves. Their fee was usually one dollar. The city got only the taxes on the building and the land.

Local government regulated the whole operation to make

sure it wasn't tainted with corruption, diseased, or controlled by undesirable people. Girls had to register with the police, as did the brothel owners. Because it was legal and controlled, the problems of juvenile delinquency, rape, white slave trading, and assorted moral problems were averted, and substantially reduced.

The county commissioners realized in their infinite wisdom that if prostitution were banned it would just go into hiding, not disappear. The needs of miners, loggers, truckers, servicemen, ranchers, sheepherders, travelling salesmen, and countless others would still have to be met. Underground and uncontrolled, it would become ugly. Street girls and their partners can become vicious real fast. And disease would become epidemic in proportion.

In Nevada prositution had always been socially useful. There were incomes for women, profits for the landlord, fees for doctors, taxes for the community, and the men were serviced. The customer satisfied his emotional and biological needs, and there was no graft or corruption. The women were friendlier and didn't have to worry about being busted, and neither did the customer. A visit to any one of Nevada's legal cathouses should bear that out to be true. As one lovely lady explained, "Without choice there is no freedom."

Conclusion

The new modern brothel has been brought out of the Dark Ages. It's clean and contemporary. It doesn't involve pimps, ripoffs, or disease. It's a free spirited business of pleasure, completely regulated, and it's legal. Logic shows it to be a better alternative to the bankrupt beliefs, hypocrisy, and immorality of those people who make it a crime.

The objective at the cathouse is to provide an enjoyable service wherein the customer is satisfied for his money spent, and hopefully will come back again. Women everywhere are playing the same game (sex for something), and men are paying for it one way or another, either in time or money, or in some other form of involvement or commitment. At a cathouse you know what you're getting, and where the commitment ends.

It's not a case of morality, or irrational sexual fears. Sex is a theater here, and it's either good theater or bad. If you want a girl to tug on your ears while you're experiencing orgasm and say to you, "You naughty boy, you naughty, naughty boy, why aren't you in school?" this is the place to come. If you want some woman to pull beads from your buttocks or whip you with a wet noodle, then that's the place to be. If you want to be with a woman who has shaved her pubic hairs into the shape of a soft cushiony heart, chances are good you'll find her in one of these houses. If you're tired of looking at your smegma-encrusted sheets and jammies due to nocturnal pollutions, or your wife or girlfriend is a piscean necrophile in bed, and seems to render her conjugal duties with great burden, the cathouse is the place for you. Sex in a cathouse can save relationships. At least it can save your sanity.

It's not really a case of morality because what consenting adults do in private is their right, and no one else's business. There are no absolutes in morality, but when we start restricting the freedom of expression of others we also restrict it for ourselves. We tend to become immoral when we dictate our moral convictions to others.

The people of Nevada have had a long history of pursuing freedom. Freedom of expression, freedom of choice to do what they want, with whom they want.

Prostitution has always been based on socio-economic demands. It follows the laws of supply and demand, and where it has been made illegal the effort has not succeeded in making man more virtuous, nor has it eradicated venereal disease. For those people who find it difficult to have normal sexual relations it serves a purpose. For those men with cosmetic or physical handicaps it serves a purpose; as well as for those men with sexual desires that cannot be satisfied "normally," or with one's current sexual partner(s). Also, men who are sexually isolated for given periods of time (through military commitments, commercial travelling, etc.) have come to appreciate the cathouse.

And what about the woman? The prostitute? The person that barters her body indiscriminately for money or gifts? Is she any different than the woman who probably would not continue to live with a man if the materialistic

160

considerations were to cease? How symbolic of love and appreciation is a new car, or jewels, or furs to the old lady. It all counts. Sexual relationships are based on economic factors, and commodity exchanges.

For many women prostitution is a solution to the economic crisis in their lives. In our patriarchal society women are taught to be dependent on males. They are usually discriminated against in employment and salary. For many, prostitution has become a lucrative alternative that gives them independence. For many it has become the solution.

One final note here: Once upon a time indiscriminate, promiscuous sex was meant to be fun. Today it can literally kill you. The sexual marketplace contains everything from your basic non-specific urethruritis (which sounds socially more acceptable than gonorrhea or syphilis), to lesions for life from herpes, to the dreaded and deadly AIDS virus.

AIDS isn't just for homosexuals, drug users, or poor people from Haiti or Africa. It doesn't respect wealth or social status. And approximately 4% of all newly reported AIDS cases stem from heterosexual intercourse. Men who have been infected with AIDS either through drug use or sexual intercourse can pass the disease along, or can prevent the spread of it through safe sexual practices.

CONTRACEPTIVES ARE A PART OF SAFE SEXUAL PRACTICE! In Nevada brothels contraceptives are considered a part of safe sexual practice, and they are mandatory. You should be glad that they are provided to you at no extra charge, because they can virtually assure you a pleasurable and risk free sexual experience when used properly. Contraceptives mean safe sex for both partners, without viral consequences.

Sex Glossary

Abolene Creme: Better than K-Y Jelly or Vaseline.

Alka-Seltzer: Sexual act performed by women inserting a moistened piece of alka seltzer in her, intending to create a fizzy climax.

Ambergris: An aphrodisiac, thought to be formed by the feces of the sperm whale impacted around a core of solid matter such as squid beaks.

Anaesthesia Sexualis: Absence of sexual feeling.

Aphrodisiacs: Sexual stimulants such as Horn of Rhino, erect penis of horse cooked highly spiced and served in a cream sauce; smoked camel hump; cantharides (such as Spanish Fly)

Apparatus Drive: On the menu at Salt Wells Villa

Arm & Hammer Baking Soda: Removes all body odor when applied to the body.

Around the World: Reaming your buttock and rectum with her tongue (after she applies Arm & Hammer Baking Soda to it!)

B/D: Bondage and Discipline (on certain menus).

Bestiality: Sex with animals.

Binaca Blast: Woman performing oral sex with her mouth full of Binaca, cool and refreshing!

Booga-Booga: Term used to describe the sexual act in primitive societies.

Brothel Sprout: One who is burned out, been in the business too long. Vegetated, cynical.

Cantharides: "Spanish Fly," formerly used as an aphrodisiac, later outlawed when too many women killed themselves on gearshift knobs of cars, after being driven mad by carnal, lustful desires.

Colored showers: Raincoat jobs, urinating on your sex partner. A.K.A. "Golden Showers."

Creme de Menthe French: Oral sex, with a smattering of creme de menthe liquor in the woman's mouth to stimulate and refresh the male.

Cribs: Little cubicles with kitchens and parlors where men would meet women for sexual purposes.

Cunnulingus: Oral sex performed on the woman.

Cunnus: Latin for female organ.

Dicteria: Greek house of prostitution (c. 500 B.C.).

Dyspareunia: Painful intercourse.

English: Whipping, especially with riding crop, quirt, taws, etc.

Eunuch: Castrated man, deprived of testes or genitalia.

French: Orally stimulate the sexual organs.

Fellatio: Oral stimulation of man's pleasure weapon.

Fellatrice: One skilled at fellatio.

Fetishists: Individual whose sexual interests are concentrated exclusively on certain parts of the body, or on certain portions of the attire.

Fundament: Underlying ground, buttocks, anus.

Golden Shower: Urinating on partner.

Greek: Anal worship, penetration (Socrates Pleasures.)

Half and Half: Half oral sex, half straight lay.

Hedonism: The doctrine that pleasure or happiness is the sole or chief goal in life.

Hereditary Taint: Missing a few of the critical ones by right of birth.

Hetaerae: Independent courtesans of the most expensive class. Comparable to a "call girl" today.

Hookers: Named in honor of Joseph Hooker (1814-1879), "Fighting Joe," Brigadier General during the Civil War, known for restoring Union Army's combat spirit by supplying his troops with "charity ladies," who became known as "Hookers." He died on Halloween.

Hyperesthesia: Abnormally increased sexual desire.

Kermit the Frog Style: Sex with the woman positioned on top, with her knees almost above her shoulders.

Knouts: Whips for flogging criminals.

Koprolagnia: The impulse to perform disgusting acts by mortifying the senses of sight, smell, taste, and hearing.

Krauses End Bulbs: The sensuous internal surface of the sex organs, (5,000+) extremely sensitive to stimulation, and located mainly in penis, clitoris, and lips.

Lingus: Latin for tongue.

Masochist: The person on the bottom of the pile.

Merkin: A pubic hair wig (rug) often times used for theatrical purposes.

Nates: Buttocks

Nay Nays: Milk Cans, Bazooms, Fun Bags, Num-Nums, Moo-Moos, Twin Doves, Snowy Hillocks, Teats, Curves.

Necrophilia: Obsession with erotic interest or stimulation with corpses.

Nymphomania: Sexual hypersensitivity where ethics and will power lose their controlling influence entirely.

Onanism: The practice of becoming intimate with oneself.

Pearl Necklace: Sexual activity involving the man placing his tumescent love club between a woman's breasts, then rocking gently back and forth culminating in ejaculation of his pearl drops love beads around her neck from his wank-wank sack bag.

Pedophile: A person who seeks sexual gratification from children.

Mr. Prolong: An odorless, tasteless, greaseless compound used externally as a topical anesthetic in a specially designed vanishing cream, for those who come too quick.

Priapism: Suffering from a continual hard on.

Quirt: A riding whip with a short handle and a raw hide lash.

Roman: Inclined to orgy.

Sodomy: Knowing carnally any male or female, any animal or bird by the anus or with the mouth or tongue; also, one who shall attempt intercourse with a dead body is guilty of sodomy and necrophilia.

Socrates: Greek style; up the fundament.

Time Utilization Factor: How much money a girl in a house makes depends on how much she charges, and how long it takes.

Turn Out: One who has just become a prostitute. A Novice.

Water sports: Enemas, urine.

Wind, Rain, & Lava: Sex act involving being blown (or farted on), then pissed on, then finally shat upon with excreta.

Index by Town

Index by Cathouse Name

171

Notes

Notes

Notes

Notes

Autographs

Autographs

Autographs

Ratings List

_____
_____
_____
_____

_____
_____
_____
_____

_____
_____
_____
_____

_____
_____
_____
_____

Numbers to Remember

_____

_____

_____

_____

_____

_____

_____

_____

_____

_____

_____

_____

_____

_____

_____

Order Form

J.R. Schwartz is pleased to offer you the following mail-order items:

Autographed copies of *The Official Guide to the Best Cat Houses in Nevada,* personally autographed by the author, J.R. Schwartz, in bold red felt tip ink and one sex pleasure menu and one pack of matches from the wildest cathouses in Nevada for $14.95!

Fill out the special order form below, and we will send your order post haste. Sorry, no C.O.D.'s accepted.

J.R., please send me the following:

_____ The book, one sex pleasure menu and one pack of matches from real cathouses in Nevada for $14.95

Enclose $2.00 additional per order to cover postage and handling (and Idaho residents please add 5% sales tax).

Enclosed is $ _____ in cash, check, or money order as payment in full for all merchandise ordered above.

I understand that I may return any and all items for a complete refund if for any reason I'm not satisifed.

Name: _____

Address: _____

City: _____ State: _____ Zip: _____

MAIL TO: J.R. SCHWARTZ,
BOX 1810
BOISE, IDAHO 83701-1810